Praise Him in the Dance

Praise Him in the Dance

by

ANNE LONG

HODDER AND STOUGHTON
LONDON SYDNEY AUCKLAND TORONTO

The author and publishers gratefully make acknowledgment to Hilary Brand, John Harwood, Martin Hulbert, The Sacred Dance Group and The Cedar of Lebanon Christian Dance Group (choreographer Janet Randell, photographers Jerry Leon and Jon Lee) for photographs of dance and dance drama; to Margaret Evening, Anne Henderson and Rosalind Patterson for songs; and to Beryl Bates and Ann Dunt for poems.

To
Mother and Father
who encouraged me into
much of life's movement and rhythm

Foreword

by Angela Hardcastle, F.I.S.T.D.

Part-time ballet mistress to the English National Opera Movement Group and teacher at Bellairs Studio, Guildford, Brooking School of Ballet, London, and Laban Art of Movement Centre, Weybridge. Freelance choreographer. Secretary of LEAP, dancers' fellowship of Arts Centre Group.

The beauties of nature lie not only in colour and sound, texture and perfume, but also in motion. To see long grass blowing in the wind, antelopes leaping, a seagull gliding or a boiling sea breaking on rocks is to know for sure that God invented movement. The Great Lover is also the Great Dancer. It follows that man, created by God in his image, with a mind and a spirit capable of conscious love and worship, has potentially the greatest beauty of movement and expression in the created world.

IF EVER THERE is a way of worshipping our God in which at present we are "peering at his reflection in a poor mirror" (1 Corinthians 13:12, *Living Bible*) it is in the use of dance in praise and prayer. Speaking as a dancer who has been a Christian for over eleven years I am sad and ashamed at my own lack of development in this area up to now. But God is teaching me and many others how the physical body he has given me (the *only* means of expressing myself on earth) may rightly, reverently and joyfully be used to express love for him. He is showing us that movement used for teaching within the church is able to communicate deeply and directly, with the whole person, to the whole person—emotions, mind, body and spirit. Old Testament prayer-life is full of it and many other cultures have given it a central place in their spiritual celebrations. We in the modern Western world have to re-learn dance in this context. The two areas of worship and teaching are the joint themes of this book.

I first met Anne Long when she contacted me 'out of the blue' after reading a letter of mine in the Christian press (part of which is quoted above). She asked me to come and help as dance adviser at a Scripture Union Communications Course, which I duly did, though in some trepidation, never having met with Christian dance drama in this form before. The course was held again the following year and, because Anne asked me to dance in the resulting presentation, it proved to be my first experience of dancing not for my own ego or to an audience but for God and in the Spirit's strength. I am still learning how to give back to God the skills, talent and training he has allowed me, by taking part in various dance events in church.

The doing of my daily work for God is another part of this subject, as I am a teacher of dance and a choreographer. But this book is not for those specialising in the performing arts for a living. It is intended for groups within Christian churches, colleges, schools and fellowships of all kinds as a practical guide to the formation and leadership of such groups, who want to praise God with their bodies in the dance, as well as in music, drama, poetry, etc. It does not tell you how to become a dancer in the professional sense, nor does it urge any and every Christian with energy to jump on a bandwagon labelled "Arts in Worship—every good church should push them"!

This book is a harvesting of the work Anne Long has been doing patiently and humbly over the last few years and the wide experience she has gained in this field. Like the author, it has an air of gentleness, love in the Spirit, joy in God's Word and in his healing and teaching ministry among his people. No script appears that has not grown up with much prayer and preparation and been submitted to the threshing-floor of Bible study, group discussion and exploration. The ideas are suitable for use in long or short workshop sessions as well as in public performance, but the emphasis in the latter is on sharing and teaching among performers and audience alike, particularly in times of worship. There is nothing 'wrong' with theatrical performance by professional players who are applauded for their abilities as well as their material; at the same time there is everything wrong with a presentation by Christians 'to the glory of God' and the embarrassment of everyone else! The aim of this book is to give practical advice on the discipline, hard work and personal commitment necessary for those who want to worship God in this way, finding out more about Christ's reality in their lives and sharing that finding with others. The Word must be clear, the dedication of work and people to God total, the offering the best possible under the Son.

After a discussion of dance and drama as communication, Anne Long goes on to deal with the organ of expression—the group— delicate and finely sensitive, training itself to become ever more expressive. This leads to the emergence of gifts (note the implication that they were there all the time and just needed some 'loving shoving' to bring them out into the light!). Chapter 3 deals with the essential and often neglected warming-up of muscles and joints and the extension of the range of movement by improvisation. Exercises calculated to banish waffle impose the limitations of rhythm, effort, quality, shape, etc., and, for improvisation, a specific task plus aids to the imagination. The dance involved in performance usually takes the simplest forms except where fully trained people are available. Material is geared to ability and mutual criticism encouraged. Do you need ideas to 'get you going'? Here are suggested themes and sources, advice on the conduct of workshops, and full-length scripts already tried and tested which, sensitively handled, give a firm basis for experiment and presentation and will help you to write and perform your own.

In *The Gospel According to Peanuts*, Robert L. Short says: "The approach of Christ to winning men . . . was to remould . . . partly through a very *human* kind of love—the lives of his disciples into works of art, through which the gentleness and kindness of their own love also was calculated to bring men to a saving knowledge of the love of God." This same approach shines through this book and the work described, in which the Holy Spirit is seen accomplishing deep healing and releasing men and women in a new way to *Praise Him in the Dance*.

Contents

Illustrations

Credits

1 Janet Randell
2 John Harwood
3 Hilary Brand

4 Martin Hulbert
5 Jon Lee and Jerry Leon
6 Sacred Dance Group

Introduction

AN INCREASING NUMBER of churches today are discovering a refreshing upsurge of creativity in their worship and life together. Especially is this evident in those places where, often through charismatic renewal, God's Spirit is leading Christians in such ways that they want, with every part of their being, to praise God and to communicate his Gospel effectively in truth and power. Through words, music, art, drama and dance, Christians are re-discovering areas of creativity and learning how to enjoy and use them. Many are also finding new and growing freedoms in themselves to be expressive in sharing God's truth.

It is primarily with church groups in mind that this book has been written, though I hope it may also find a wider use in Christian workshops and houseparties, colleges and schools. It is not intended for professionals but for those amateurs who want to explore the possibilities of using drama and dance in the context of the Bible and its teaching. My hope is that it will provide guidelines and ideas for groups who want to work and learn together using these media. Some may want to dramatise a Bible narrative to include in a Sunday service, whilst others may want to discover ways of introducing dances of praise into the pattern of church worship. Some will, inevitably, doubt the rightness of such activities. I have attempted to look truthfully at some of those doubts in chapter 1, but the rest of the book is very practical, containing exercises, ideas, shorter and longer scripts. I hope, too, that some will become convinced of the value and potential of drama and dance for biblical teaching in visual form.

Some of the material used here emerged from a group originally made up of Christian students at Gipsy Hill College of Education. Over a period of three years we worked together to communicate Christian teaching through drama and dance. We often struggled to discover right ways of using movement, words and music to teach God's truth with integrity. And in the struggling we found ourselves learning not only about communication but also about relationships, mutual love, prayer and personal growth. I am deeply grateful to the Charis Group and my co-producer, Margaret Evening, for a wonderful time of learning together. As we worked, prayed, sifted ideas, rehearsed, then visited churches to enact the Gospel teaching, so we found God and his Word increasingly true, vital and relevant. Since then I have been involved in numerous workshops and parish weekends where we have worked together to explore biblical material and present it in services for teaching and worship.

One danger of attempting to put live ideas and scripts into book form is that they will be taken up too quickly without due consideration of the particular situation or group concerned and thereby lose their vitality. What is exactly right for one situation is not necessarily so for another. Much of the improvised drama and dance currently appearing has a freedom about it which would be lost if it were captured between book covers. If the longer scripts included in this book prove right for certain situations, and if they speak to participants and observers, then I am pleased. But I shall be even more delighted if the ideas and improvisations included here lead people on to seek and discover, through prayer and practice, fresh ways of sharing God's Word in their own situations and churches.

In addition to expressing gratitude to the Charis Group, I want also to thank others who have encouraged me in the writing of this book. To Margaret Evening go special thanks. We worked together with Charis and from her I learnt an openness and flexibility which made our sharing in production an increasing pleasure instead of a threat. We worked together on scripts and to her I owe thanks for much of the original plan for this book, many ideas in it and especially for the major contributions she made to the longer script, "With Love from Jesus" in chapter 8, and to the Unity dance drama in chapter 6. Angela Hardcastle, with her expertise as a professional dancer and teacher, has generously advised and helped me with a graciousness which always inspired and never depressed. Anne Greig, who so skilfully and patiently typed the manuscript, also exercised a ministry of encouragement which was supportive at times when the work was uphill. My thanks are also due to Stella Mayes and Penny Dowgill for their help with some of the dances described in chapter 7. Colin Buchanan gave valued help with proofs and many other friends from St. John's College gave the prayers, support and patience which brought this book to completion. I am grateful to them.

Anne Long
Nottingham, 1975

CHAPTER I

Drama and Dance in Christian Worship

WHAT PLACE SHOULD the arts have in the Christian life and to what extent should the Church become involved in them? For centuries there has been much ambivalence amongst Christians in their attitudes to the arts. At certain periods in church history there has been a flourishing of creativity and at other times a withdrawal— for good and bad reasons. Many have tended to leave the arts on the sideline, considering other things to be more important. They may be right for themselves but are wrong if they declare their personal priorities to be normative. Francis Schaeffer writes: "The arts and the sciences do have a place in the Christian life—they are not peripheral. For a Christian, redeemed by the work of Christ and living within the norms of Scripture and under the leadership of the Holy Spirit, the Lordship of Christ should include an interest in the arts. A Christian should use these arts to the glory of God, not just as tracts, mind you, but as things of beauty to the praise of God."[1]

At present there is considerable interest in, and, on the whole, more acceptance of, the visual arts, music and music-making, drama and dance. Many churches have groups who contribute regularly to services, though standards vary considerably. In some places there is genuine talent, hard work and thinking in an endeavour to find true Christian forms and valid content. In other places, partly through lack of teaching, the results are second-rate, well-intentioned but lacking in true Christian understanding. As with other areas of our Christian living, so our creativity and gifts also have to undergo a kind of death and resurrection.

The use of drama and dance in church provokes valid questions.

Most of this book is very practical, introducing a range of ideas, suggestions and scripts. In this first chapter we shall look at some of the questions which people may well be asking about the use of these media in a church setting.

 ## 1. CREATIVITY

God is Creator and made us in his image and likeness. One feature of that likeness is that we too are potentially creative, whether we have discovered this or not. Creativity is part of the privilege of our humanity. Some people have had little or no opportunity to discover this. Others feel there is little they can 'do', though they appreciate listening to music, walking in an art gallery or reading poetry. Others again may have learnt an instrument once, passed 'O' level art, sung in the school choir or performed in the school play. Some shyly admit they sometimes write verse or songs for their own enjoyment. Amongst many Christians there is both evident and hidden potential which, given training and encouragement, can be used in the church to God's glory and the help and teaching of people. The pity is that so often there is neither training nor encouragement offered and consequently our church services often lack that life, creativity and colour which should characterise the worship of God. Whilst we repress our God-given creativity we are not showing each other or those outside the church the life and beauty of our Creator. We both limit Christ's Lordship and appear closed up, half alive, unable to give ourselves fully, gladly and with all our being to the worship of God. By comparison, when the Holy Spirit is free to move in us, he opens up new areas of creativity, giving new space, freedoms and gifts.

Drama and dance are only two particular expressions of creativity, whose value some Christians might doubt, especially in the context of church worship. "Surely the church is not the place for acting and dancing?" Some may think such activities are intrinsically 'wrong' or 'bad'. Probably most would agree that they are legitimate means of expression in themselves but that the important question is, how are they to be used? If used without integrity, or springing from a false view of man, or propagating untruth, they are clearly not suited to the worship of God. Used with integrity and truth they can take their place in the worship and teaching ministry of the Church. Drama and dance are communicative arts. In different ways they 'speak'. If they speak what is true in such a way that people can consider, understand, learn, remember and grow in Christian understanding, then they are of value. I am in no way suggesting they displace preaching, though they may well be used to underline and reinforce it. But, used wisely, they can become a legitimate part of church worship and learning.

2. DRAMA AND DANCE IN THE BIBLE

What place does the Bible give to drama and dance and their use in worship?

In the Old Testament, dance is a feature of Israelite worship, especially the chief annual festivals which were special times of corporate religious celebration. W. O. E. Oesterley in *The Sacred Dance* enumerates at least eight varieties of dance in the Old Testament used on different occasions.[2] The Hebrew word most frequently used is '*hul*' meaning to dance or whirl. It is a word suggesting vigorous dancing. Occasionally the word '*raqad*' is used, meaning to dance, skip or leap. We know that singing and a variety of instruments were used with the dancing—hand-drums, castanets, various kinds of pipes, harps, lutes, lyres, cymbals and the large rams' horns. It would seem as if their praises were quite vigorous!

The prophetess Miriam danced with other women to timbrel and song after the triumphant crossing of the Red Sea (Exodus 15:20, 21). David "danced before the Lord with all his might" (2 Samuel 6:14) as the ark of God was brought triumphantly back to Jerusalem. Jephthah's daughters danced to the timbrel (Judges 11:34). The psalmist exhorted God's people to "praise his name with dancing" (Psalm 149:3) and to "praise him with timbrel and dance" (Psalm 150:4), whilst the singers and dancers who celebrated Zion, the city of God, confessed this place to be the source of life and refreshing, "All my springs are in you". In Psalm 30 the psalmist changed from his mourning rites and clothing to dancing and festal garments, "Thou hast turned for me my mourning into dancing". In Ecclesiastes the writer said there was

both "a time to mourn, and a time to dance". With the destruction
of Jerusalem and its temple in 586 B.C. the joyful worship of the
people was turned from dancing to mourning (Lamentations 5:15)
but the promise was given in Jeremiah 31:13 that their fortunes
would be reversed, "Then shall the maidens rejoice in the dance,
and the young men and the old shall be merry". These references
show the sense of joy that the Israelites expressed in their worship.
Their God was alive and active on their behalf. "The jubilant
dancing is the measure of what [God's] action means to the
pilgrims. He has come into the midst as Saviour. What feet can
be still?" (J. H. Eaton)[3]

There were also occasions (see Exodus 32:19 and Job 21:11)
when the dance was not directed towards God and the merry-
making became a part of degenerate revels.

Although we cannot give chapter and verse of drama scripts in
the Old Testament, we can still rightly use the word 'drama' for
many of its events. The tabernacle worship contained much
symbolism which was a powerful acting out. The priest was
instructed, when anyone made an animal offering to God, to throw
the blood against the altar, prepare the fire, lay out the pieces of
flesh, etc. Different kinds of offerings were to be made to God—
the sin offering, the cereal offering, the peace offering and others.
The considerable amount of ceremonial that had to take place
was a powerful demonstration to the people of the seriousness of
sin and the holiness of God. The purpose of these rituals was that
the people might be helped to understand the character of God
and their relationship to him. The ceremonial for the Day of
Atonement was similarly dramatic. Read Leviticus chapter 16
and imagine the occasion, especially as Aaron laid his hands upon
the goat, confessing over it Israel's sins, transferring them to the
beast and driving it out into the wilderness.

For another kind of drama, a bizarre and symbolic enactment,
we can look at Ezekiel. The messages of judgment and doom he
was required to share with the people before the fall of Jerusalem
were going to be difficult to communicate. The siege, subsequent
famine and destruction were prophetically acted out by the prophet
—probably in the open space in front of his house—in such a way
that bystanders would inevitably be gripped. He set the stage for
the siege of Jerusalem with a large brick model, then daily lay
down on his side facing the model, his arm bared and his body

bound. He cut, weighed and divided his hair to portray the destruction of the city's inhabitants. Here was high drama, poignantly prophetic, used by God to warn the people and show them the consequences of their sins.

In the New Testament there is no evidence of the dance and music-making that characterised Israelite worship. This may be, partly, because the first Christians met in houses where there would hardly be space to dance. Certainly there is no injunction against dancing. There is one clear example of dance which was in no way glorifying to God. The daughter of Herodias, wife of King Herod, danced before him in such a way that he rashly promised her anything she asked for. Prompted by her mother, she asked for the head of John the Baptist and the request was granted. As with the two Old Testament examples of wanton dancing, it is clear that the orientation and content of dance can direct attention either towards or away from God. The difference between the two is considerable and the consequences indicate that there is an important element of responsibility in public performance. What we see and become involved in inevitably motivate our actions and behaviour.

Yet even if there are no examples of New Testament dance and drama as such to discuss, we must still look at some of the outstanding ways in which Jesus taught and involved his hearers in learning. In his use of parables there is a quality of immediacy which quickly arrested the attention of those who listened, whether at a deep or superficial level. "Hear then the parable of the sower," he began. At once his audience had a clear pictorial reference point within their own culture. All of the parables described in Matthew chapter 13 mirror the contemporary lifestyle of the listeners. How could they help but be involved?

Jesus also used visual aids with a dramatic immediacy which brought the lesson right home. "Show me the money for the tax," he said, and they brought him a coin (Matthew 22:19). He did not simply invite them to think about or imagine a coin but held one in his hand, using it to demonstrate his point. Similarly he brought a child, probably by the hand, into the midst of his disciples and used him or her to teach them about humility. The miracles he performed—such as the feeding of the five thousand—were powerful and dramatic enactments of the Kingdom. He used Moses's symbolic drama of the bronze serpent on a pole (Numbers

21:6–9) as an illustration of his forthcoming crucifixion (John 3:14, 15). He involved his hearers in his teaching in a way that might shock some present-day congregations. Relating the story of the Good Samaritan to a lawyer (Luke 10:25–37), he suddenly zoomed in with a very direct question: "Which of these three, do you think, proved neighbour to the man who fell among the robbers?" Jesus was both involving the lawyer and providing an opportunity for immediate feed-back to see if he really had understood the point of the narrative. Not surprisingly, he had. On another occasion, Jesus used a parable about a vineyard hired out to tenants (Matthew 21:33–43). At the climax of the story he asked his hearers to give their verdict on the wicked tenants—what would the owner do with them? Thoroughly involved in the narrative, they answered immediately and with great feeling, "He will put those wretches to a miserable death." Then, with poignant drama, Jesus brought the point right home—they themselves were the wretches they had just condemned. The point was not lost, we read in v. 45. Certainly, in his teaching methods Jesus used a dramatic context, technique and application which made his message very difficult to avoid. Can we learn from this in our Bible-teaching methods today?

Finally, let us look at an example where Jesus used a dramatic occasion for his own ends, heightening the drama by his timed entrance and speech. John chapter 7 sets the scene at the Jewish feast of Tabernacles. It lasted seven days and, as well as being a kind of harvest festival, also commemorated God's provision for his people in their wilderness wanderings. Part of the ceremonial was that each day the people marched around the great altar whilst the priest went to the Pool of Siloam and filled one of the temple pitchers with water. He carried it back whilst the people recited responses, then poured the water out on the altar as an offering to God. This was a vivid reminder of God's provision of water, even from a rock in the wilderness, and an enacted prayer for the continuing of his blessings. On the last day of the ceremony, the people marched around the altar seven times, commemorating the march round Jericho when the walls fell and the city was taken. It was this setting Jesus chose for his proclamation that if anyone was thirsty in spirit, he himself was the source of living water (vv. 37, 38). What a master-stroke of dramatic timing, entrance and climax! Not surprisingly there was a reaction.

So we see how Jesus's methods had a quality of immediacy and drama, highlighting his skill and resources as a teacher. These examples do not therefore legitimise *all* drama and *every* dramatic form we try to use in Christian communication, but they reveal a rich variety of method which we ought to become aware of and learn from in our presentation of God's truth.

3. DEVELOPMENTS

After the New Testament period there seems to be no evidence for dance or dramatic presentation until the fourth century when we know it took place in some churches though, later, Augustine spoke out against it because of its association with pagan festivities. The Middle Ages saw the advent of the Miracle and Morality plays which proved extremely popular. Some of the plays, if not all, brought biblical teaching from inside the church building out into the churchyard, streets and squares. Perhaps it was almost inevitable that truth often became mixed with fable and colourful, if not always accurate, interpretations of the Bible. Yet the enthusiasm with which many of the clergy and laity greeted these presentations gives us a clue as to the potential of such a teaching method.

Attitudes towards the dance varied. Some clergy thought it was entirely inappropriate to church worship whereas others were prepared to allow it with the hope of controlling its use. After the Reformation, although attacked by many, it did not entirely disappear. It was hardly surprising that the Puritans denounced such activity, for much dance and drama had lapsed into lasciviousness. In the Victorian era many decried self-expression, considering it to be in bad taste. Undoubtedly some of this rejection of the arts by the Church stemmed from a loss of true content and form and a consequent abuse, but there was also, on the part of many, much negative thinking about the human body.

In these days there is a resurgence of interest in dance and drama in the context of worship. This is evident in a wide spectrum of churches, denominations and countries. There is a growing number of liturgical dance groups, and some of our cathedrals, such as Coventry, Leicester, Southwark, St. Paul's and Westminster Abbey have included dance and drama in their worship and festivals. Local churches are also producing their own home-grown groups and this has been a notable feature of churches where charismatic renewal has brought fresh surges of creativity. St. Michael-le-Belfry, York, uses dance in worship; St. Thomas, Crookes in Sheffield, is using street theatre where the Bible is taken into the streets in dramatic form. The Millmead Baptist Church in Guildford made a moving contribution in drama with their home-grown "Children of the King" and St. Stephen's, Twickenham, includes dance and dance drama in its worship. These are only a few examples of the many churches where these things are happening and where, encouraged by workshops and symposia, people are being taught how to incorporate dance and drama into their patterns of worship.

4. OBJECTIONS AND QUESTIONS

(a) *"Are dance and drama distractions to worship?"*

What is worship? One definition is "the distinctive agenda of the church when it meets". That agenda will include praying, singing, preaching, reading the Scriptures. The direction is two-fold—from God to man, involving a receiving, and from man to God, involving an offering. This offering is man's response to God, a response that can assume different expressions. Singing can be part of that response whereby people praise God in music, and words and dancing can also be part of it, whereby some praise God using the language of the body. The proclamation of the Word will be a means of people receiving God's truth as will also be the reading of the Bible. A dramatisation of biblical material can also be a legitimate means of receiving God's truth. Held within this context, rather than being seen as separate 'items', dance and drama need not become distractions but rather can be reinforcements to biblical praising and teaching, so long as they are properly worked out and integrated. They can, if rightly used, become vehicles of teaching, presenting God's Word visually and reinforcing the verbal statement. Or, as one Christian teacher of dance put it, they can be "like windows, offering a clearer view of God's truth".

Some people's objections may well rest upon their preconceived (and maybe prejudiced) ideas of what church worship should and should not be. There are those who are very scared of anything moving in a service—either emotionally (such as the sermon), or physically (such as the kiss of peace or a dance). Some want a service that is safe and completely predictable where they can keep their liturgical masks in position and not relate to others. Certainly meeting each other in the presence of God can be very embarrassing if people are unsure about either God or each other. Mask-wearing can, especially if encouraged, become a rationalised defence against the reality of meeting God and others as we are, without cover. I am not suggesting that we seek after novelty in our patterns of worship but neither should we settle for an attitude that "what has always been must therefore continue to be". Let us not confuse the essential permanence of the truths of God with some of the means of communication of those truths, for whose permanence there is no scriptural authority. Worship is a living activity and if changes sometimes offer a threat to our personal sense of security, this does not necessarily make those changes wrong.

(b) "Is drama just play-acting and pretence?"

It is true that the Greek word for 'actor' also gives us our English words 'hypocrite' and 'pretender'. What place could these words possibly have in the context of Christian worship? 'Play-acting' has about it a negative connotation, and 'pretending' speaks of that which is less than real, which does not sound like a good mix with Christianity.

Certainly the whole area of identification in the portrayal of character needs to be carefully thought through by Christians engaged in acting. The principal of a well-known drama school once said that he considered Christians found this a more problematic area than non-Christians since the Christian model is Christ himself and to keep assuming other character roles could produce great conflict in the person. Unless some degree of objectivity is retained by an actor when he identifies with the character he is playing, he could lose his own personal identity and discover there was nothing left of his true self. But, given that degree of objectivity, 'pretence' in acting is not wrong (unless used to promote deliberate perversion). Chapter 2 section 4 includes an example of dramatic identification.

But there is also a positive connotation to 'pretending'. We can 'pretend' towards that which we want to become before we have fully attained it. Those who join in the liturgical response about "walking before him in holiness and righteousness all the days of our life" hope, as they regularly repeat the words, to attain the state described. Those who say "Praise the Lord!" hope, through repetition of the phrase, to let it become increasingly a habit of life. In this sense 'play acting' can be used in a positive sense as the person seeks to assume the character he is portraying.

(c) "Do dance and drama encourage Christians to focus wrongly on the physical?"

Here is a question to which a quick answer cannot be given. There has been, and still is, some confused thinking amongst Christians about the body. Some Christian thinking and teaching still encourage people to believe that their minds and spirits are far superior to their bodies, about which little need be said. But things do need to be said if we are to understand and live out the biblical teaching on our humanity.

This attitude, which wrongly fragments the nature of man, has its roots in Platonic dualism. The Greek philosopher Plato regarded the physical body as a defilement to the soul, a prison-house in which the soul lay captive until death gave release. Much of this attitude crept into Christian thinking and it is important to see that its origins are not biblical. The Hebrew doctrine of man stresses a unity of the spiritual and the physical. In the New Testament, although a right emphasis is given to bodily discipline, there is no despising of the body. Rather, Paul teaches, "The body is not meant for immorality, but for the Lord, and the Lord for the body" (1 Corinthians 6:13). Our bodies are not unfortunate extras but part of that humanity with which we are to glorify God. We are not to hate our own flesh but "nourish" and "cherish" it "as Christ does the Church" (Ephesians 5:29). Christian belief in the Incarnation also establishes the value of the body for "the Word was made flesh". At the resurrection the physical body will no longer be operative but a new, spiritual body will be given.

"A Church which believes in the resurrection of the body cannot rest content with a life-style that deadens the body. A Church which believes in the unity of body and soul must do all it can to declare the redemption that overcomes the dichotomy between them." (Professor J. G. Davies)[4]

This is not to suggest that an exaggerated estimate be put on the body but rather that a true integration be sought between man's mind, emotions, spirit and body.

When a right respect is found for the different parts and their functioning together, then comes integration and a growing personal integrity. Perhaps this is why Paul used his extended metaphor likening the Christian fellowship and its interdependence to a physical body with all its interrelated limbs and organs (1 Corinthians 12:14-26). It is possible for a person so to be living in the realm of his mind and cerebral activity that he becomes something of a stranger to his own body. Or, conversely, he may be so preoccupied with his body that he becomes isolated from the integrity of his mental processes. Our various parts need to be united and integrated. Quite frequently people—especially adults—feel embarrassed and even fearful when invited to express themselves in movement. I have often found in workshops that people who are well educated at the level of the mind and verbally confident and fluent, have partly lost touch with their own bodies and the ability of the body to communicate. Some say they 'feel silly' or are worried about how they look or whether they might be laughed at. Sadly, the education of the whole person can easily become unbalanced so that a highly trained mind resides in a body that has become rather a neglected stranger. But this state of affairs can change. Christ came to liberate and some people have discovered that one aspect of this liberation is that we can be set free to praise and glorify him at different and new levels. The praises of our minds and hearts can also touch our limbs and bodies!

Perhaps some people are fearful that, through watching dance or drama, especially in a church setting, sexual feelings will be aroused, and that does not feel at all right. There is nothing intrinsically 'wrong' about sexual arousal or desire—rather, it is a matter of the direction in which that desire moves. There is nothing wrong with feelings which move out in appreciation of bodies and bodily movements. But there is everything wrong with lust which greedily seizes the appreciative feelings and feeds upon them solely for self-gratification. Perhaps the subtle dividing line between these two areas lies in the realm of the imagination. Either we seek to exercise integrity and, by the light of God's truth, recognise and discipline our desires at that particular point where outgoing appreciation shifts to selfish gratification, or we let our imagination lead us into those areas of indulgence in lustful fantasies which are a mockery of true love.

It would seem, then, that the answer to the original question lies not in a wrong denial of the body and bodily expression but rather in the discovery, through personal growth and the Holy Spirit's illumination, that God desires our humanity to be integrated, with his truth reigning in our inmost being.

5. RIGHT USES

It is now worth looking at some of the positive reasons for using dance and drama in worship in order to understand why these are helpful means of expression and communication.

First, Christian truth can be watched as well as listened to. Just as the ears are an important gateway to the mind, so are the eyes. As outlined above, the body speaks and its vocabulary is movement. Later chapters will go into this in more detail. Before even a baby has learnt to talk in words and sentences, he is speaking with his body, using hands, fists, legs, postures and facial expressions in order to communicate. Children will jump for joy, shiver with excitement, bang and storm with anger, also using their bodies to reinforce their words. Adults have more means at their disposal for concealing their thoughts and feelings. Yet, even so, their bodies often communicate accurately what is going on within— the rigid tension of controlled anger, the slouch of depression, the outstretched arms of welcome, the held gaze of love. Whether it is by participating in dance and drama or watching it, there can be a portrayal of truth which can speak to people in fresh and arresting ways.

Secondly, whether by taking part or by watching, people can become really involved—and involvement is an important part of true learning. It is one thing to read a narrative, such as John 8:2–11 where Jesus forgives a woman who has been caught in adultery, and then to meditate on it and learn from it. But it can also bring a fresh dimension and understanding to become involved in what is being portrayed—the hard legalism of the Pharisees, the vulnerability of the woman and the measured actions and loving acceptance of Jesus. Involvement in the affairs of others inevitably affects our own motivation and behaviour, whether this be real-life relationships or enacted ones. Most people can think of times when, at one level, they have been listening to a talk or sermon yet, at other levels of their being, have just not been involved so that the teaching has not sunk in deeply. The 'learning by doing', so evident in our educational methods today, has rightly taken the principle of involvement seriously and encouraged teachers to provide contexts of learning as well as facts and information within those contexts. One person, on watching a dramatic portrayal of Jesus healing the lepers—a story she had read many times before—became really involved in what she saw to the point of tears. The narrative was familiar but the communication came through the eyes as well as the ears, involving her in a sequence of relationships in which people were healed. God's word entered into her at a deep level and taught her more about his healing power and its potential today. One male student in our drama group wrote: "I have always tended to be a more academically biassed person, and discovered that through the dance and drama I could also use my body as well as my mind . . . The experience was very deep for me and certainly was a tremendous help towards the academic work for the B.Ed. degree." So whether the involvement is through watching or taking part, dramatisation promotes involvement and involvement learning.

Thirdly, as outlined in the previous section, in dance and drama we are wanting to use the whole of our humanity, bodies included, to glorify God.

In recommending these means I would not want to go to the extreme of saying that everyone should use them or start forming groups. It is rather that those who want to become involved should clear their thinking as to what they are doing and why. Discipline and hard work will be needed in order to discover and exercise their creativity in a genuinely Christian way. It is not enough simply to adapt those secular forms and ideas which are part of our fallen culture and try to Christianise them by changing the words or adding an evangelistic appeal. We must go on wrestling with basic matters of form and content so that our offering to God and to people is true and valid in content, well constructed, and communicated in such a way that medium and message are complementary rather than confusing. With these goals clearly before us we can go on to use our creativity to God's glory.

CHAPTER 2

The Emergence and Life of a Group

1. FORMING A GROUP

ANY CHURCH GROUP that meets together needs to know the reason for its existence, whether it be a parish house group or the young people's fellowship committee or the church choir. Likewise, a group that comes together for dance or drama needs to be sure of what it is doing and why. Our group, numbering between thirty and forty young men and women, originally came together for Christian outreach and our objective was to share the teaching of the gospel visually and verbally through drama, dance and music. It was not a church-based group—most of those who took part were students and staff in a college of education—and the work was mostly done in term time. The group functioned together for four years, after which, by group decision, it disbanded. Most of the students and the two tutors leading the group left college and several went to churches who invited them to help with forming church-based groups. During its life together there often came the need to pause in order to clarify our goals, re-define our aims and renew our sense of direction.

In a local church a dance-drama group may come into existence for one of several reasons at a practical level. Perhaps something different is felt to be needed for a youth service or for outreach during a church mission. Perhaps the church is to be involved in an outdoor festival or wants to add a fresh dimension to its worship through dance. A group may come together temporarily or may become a more permanent part of the church's ministry. It is easy to watch a group somewhere else and enthusiastically speed back to one's own church to gather together any who might like the thought of 'having a go'. Be warned: it is much easier to jump on the bandwagon and set it in motion than to keep it going with a continuing sense of purpose and commitment. A group of this nature, really to fulfil something worthwhile, must be conscious of what it is taking on and why. As with any other church activity, there needs to be a sense of rightness and God's clear leading. Any Christian work will include times of frustration and difficulty and it is at those times we need the reassurance that God called us into that particular ministry. Maybe the opening will come through an invitation from the church leadership, maybe through the suggestion of others in the church who see what could be done, maybe through a personal prompting. However it may be, avoid rushing into it, pray about the possibilities and expect God's guidance.

It might be useful to use three questions as guide-lines for forming a group. Firstly, is this the right timing for a dance-drama group in the church? I recall one church where the curate was enthusiastic to introduce a drama group but various factors seemed to indicate that some church members would have negative reactions and the church was not yet ready for this activity. He waited for eighteen months then felt it right to go ahead and a piece of dance drama was introduced into the evening service. There was a generally warm and positive reaction and since then the group has continued with performances in the church and also in the street. If some church members are going to be unhappy and critical about innovations in services, perhaps the answer is to wait and pray rather than abandon the possibility. A second guide-line question could be, will the vicar or minister see a dance-drama group as a potential ministry within the church and will he give it his encouragement and support? This is necessary if the group hopes to be involved in teaching and worship. Thirdly, are there people in the church who seem able and wanting to commit themselves to such work? Commitment is very important and later in this chapter we shall look more closely at what it means to work in a committed way.

2. GROUP LEADERSHIP

Having looked into some preliminary aspects of starting a group, we now go on to think about leading it. Who will lead and what will be involved? There may be an 'obvious' leader/producer, such as the person who drew people together, or it may be that one of the group emerges as leader. Perhaps it is someone with experience in teaching or choreography, production or acting. If so, some of the skills available will prove very useful, though if such skills are not obviously apparent it does not necessarily mean that a group cannot function. Occasionally individuals with professional training are to be found in a church yet have never seen quite how their specialist gifts could possibly fit into church life and witness. Indeed some might feel puzzled about any possible link between their professional life in the arts and their Christian life in the church. A few might even feel disapproved of as artists by some Christians who have never had to think in depth about the relationship between their faith and the arts. Thanks to the work of groups like the Arts Centre Group, Christian Arts Project and others, this attitude is gradually giving place to a more sympathetic acceptance of the arts and their rightful place in the Church, but there is still important work to be done in this area. Paula Douthett, co-director of the Sacred Dance Group from Boulder, Colorado, had no idea of the consequences of a question put to her by the Lutheran pastor of her church. He asked her and her husband, Bill, what were their gifts and talents. Bill's gift of teaching seemed a very sensible and practical one—an asset in any church—whereas Paula answered apologetically that her only talent seemed to be dancing—and where did that fit into the church's ministry? Shortly after, the pastor asked her if she would arrange a dance for a special service in the church. Things moved on from there until there is now a group of dancers brought together by God from different churches, states and countries and now sponsored by the Boulder church for a ministry of teaching and worship to other churches and countries. Their workshops and presentations are a clear and beautiful demonstration of Christian creativity, praise and commitment to God.

However the leadership of the group becomes apparent, that person must be someone accepted and respected by the rest, otherwise there might be loss of confidence. Leadership of any group has its own demands and responsibilities and the following points are worth considering. They are not necessarily listed in order of importance.

(a) *Requirements for group leadership*

(i) The leader needs to maintain a right sense of priorities, both personally and also for the group. In a Christian group it is important to have an open relationship with God in order to be available for his leadings, teachings and creativity. As with other aspects of the group work this will mean time, availability and personal discipline. The leader's commitment to this work and the group members must be evident.

(ii) The leader needs a sense of vision with which to enthuse and lead the group—vision for the work and its content and for how it can be used.

(iii) It is very helpful if the leader has previously had some experience of production or teaching or leading a group similar to this. Clear communication and teaching skills are a great asset, especially when it comes to explaining ideas or teaching complicated routines!

(iv) But the leader/producer should also see himself as one of the dance-drama group. He is not 'set apart' and his ideas are not sacrosanct. He should be open to the rest of the group and to learning through them. Sometimes their ideas will be better than his and their criticisms valid. A good leader will not be above criticism but will rather learn how to sift and evaluate it. If certain decisions about the group work are clearly his responsibility, there will be other ones which should be seen more as group decisions. One girl in our group very much appreciated the value of shared decisions which made the group, for her, far more a unity than just a collection of individuals all 'doing their own thing'.

(v) The leader will need a growing regard for the individuals with whom he/she is working and for their differences. Sometimes this will come easily but at other times it definitely will not! In this, it is important to learn the value of encouraging people in their work. They will often re-double their efforts when really encouraged both individually and as a group.

(vi) It will be part of the leader's job to help discover and assess other people's gifts and then help them use them. There might be a wide range of undeveloped or unknown talents amongst the group, from dance and beautiful movement to technical skills or song-writing. People have far more creativity in them than often they realise or have ever had the chance to discover. This is where a good leader can give much help.

(vii) It is probably worth emphasising what is implicit throughout this book, that a great deal of hard work and overtime will need to be put in, both by leader and group members. Producing good material (especially when it is for public viewing) will involve regular, disciplined rehearsals and work together and the leader needs to be prepared for the implications of this before beginning.

(viii) The work will include the preparation and shaping of scripts but will also involve important practical matters such as studying the space available (quite a problem in some churches!), thinking of suitable music and sound effects, having at least an elementary understanding of tapes, tape recorders and the P.A. systems often, though not always, available in churches. He must also learn the best pattern for rehearsals so that time is well used. As the group works together more, so it should become increasingly possible to delegate jobs like the use of the tape recorder to others—indeed, there may well be someone in the church who is willing and able to give more expert help.

These, then, are some aspects of leadership worth considering though others will emerge as the work develops.

(b) *Shared leadership*

It is probably worthwhile mentioning the possibility of a shared leadership of the group, for we discovered it to be a very valuable and enriching way of working. It might emerge right from the beginning that there are two people gifted to work together at production or it may be—as in our case—that after the group has actually got started a second person arrives whose gifts complement and fit in with those of the original producer. With us, my colleague had more experience in movement and dance and I had done more in teaching drama. So we joined forces and the group accepted us both as co-producers. In the early days I sometimes felt threatened when our differences emerged but, as we gained confidence in each other, so the harmony increased. We found that when we really worked together in a committed way, the result was the richer, but at times when we were not communicating enough or skimped shared prayer, planning and sifting, then this inevitably affected the work of the whole group. We found it necessary to plan rehearsals together, test out script ideas with each other, discuss aims and goals and—not least important—define our different roles and contributions so that we could complement, rather than compete with, each other. This was not always as easy or objective as it might sound on paper but it provided both personal- and group-learning points which found positive repercussions in our whole work together.

3. WORKING TOGETHER

As individuals who are interested to work at drama and dance in a Christian context come together, many aspects of the task will need defining, discussing and attempting. Before looking specifically at how and where to start the actual movement (see chapter 3), it is worth looking harder at what commitment is likely to involve. There is nothing worse than starting off with an enthusiastic bunch of people then finding that attendance at rehearsals is erratic and support uneven. It is better to spell out at the beginning what commitment to this might involve rather than discover the difficulties halfway through. We found, in working creatively together, that a three-fold commitment was essential —to God, to the work we did and to each other. This might seem rather strange—indeed, we would not have been able to formulate it as clearly as this when we first got together to work out our first piece of dance drama—but it emerged as the vital thread running through the whole fabric of what we produced.

(a) *Commitment to God*

In using drama and dance to communicate truth we are using not just one part of our personality but the whole of us, body, mind and spirit. To communicate that truth truthfully we need to know where we stand in relation to it. As Christians we are to submit each part of ourselves to God for him to work in by his Spirit—and, again, this will include our bodies, minds and spirits. We are using our bodies to teach truths about God or his world or humanity, so we must be open to him in portraying and communicating those truths. St. Paul writes: "Present your bodies as a living sacrifice, holy and acceptable to God, which is your spiritual worship" (Romans 12:1), and this is how it should be with Christians working in these areas. God will be, both for the individual and the group, the focal point and centre of it all. Anne said how much she appreciated the incorporating of our dance-drama into a service of church worship "because it helped me to appreciate that we weren't a travelling circus or even an evening's entertainment, but we were directing our worship to God—though this did not mean that we weren't interested in communicating with man". The object and goal, then, were to bring glory to God the Creator and teach his truth. In doing this sort of work we found it really was necessary that the group should consist of committed Christians. This was not in order to be exclusive or an 'in-group' but because we saw unity of belief and purpose to be an important part of the communication. If, for example, some were not happy to pray together, there could be a fragmentation which would affect the whole.

We soon began to discover the priority of prayer in what we were attempting. It is not a 'desirable extra' included if and when there is time, but the essential context of all that is done. Include prayer at the start and end of all rehearsals—and sometimes in the middle too! Pray for each other, for the work in hand, for the church—both your own and anywhere you might be presenting work. Pray for musicians or narrators in the group and their compositions, learn to praise, worship God and sing together. Ask for his guidance and creativity in scripting and choreography, pray for clear communication. Remember group relationships too. It would be rather contradictory to perform a dance of unity if there were unresolved relationship difficulties within the group. We found it to be an important principle that when misunderstandings, jealousies, resentments and other hurts arose (as they inevitably do in any group, Christian or not) people saw the point of putting these right, either privately or in group discussion. This never led to a morbid 'soul-scraping' but helped us to retain an essential

unity which was not constantly being undermined by petty
squabbles. We also prayed about the requests we received to give
presentations and which ones we should accept. As the group
became better known, there came a growing number of invitations
to churches, festivals and special events. We could almost have let
it become a full-time occupation at one stage and it was important
to discover God's guidance and establish whether our contribution was likely to fit in or not. Rather than try to bend in
every direction, it is better to find out about the nature of the
occasion and whether a piece of dance or drama seems appropriate
for it. Invitations should not be accepted indiscriminately.

Does it seem like stretching a point to pray about tapes, P.A.
systems and floorboards? Yet, if we hadn't, I'm not sure where
we would have been! Few churches were ever designed to include
dance or drama and very often inconvenient screens, awkward
steps, grids in the floor and radiators dominating good floor space
make for headaches when it comes to production and staging. It
is always as well to spend time surveying the space you are going
to be using in a building and deciding how to make the most of it.
Visibility can often be a problem, though some churches have
acting blocks or a free-standing platform available. Otherwise, if
there is a school near the church, it may be possible to borrow a
few blocks from there to elevate the whole performance area or
vary levels. I found it a useful piece of advice that, instead of
grumbling about the snags of church architecture, it might be
better to thank God and ask him for eyes to see how to use the
awkward steps, narrow chancel, small space, etc., as creatively as
possible.

We also made a point of meeting together for prayer in plenty
of time before a presentation was due to begin. We often had a
short meditation from the Bible, thanksgiving, confession, then
intercession focusing on the congregation and ourselves, also some
time for silent reflection and prayer, opening ourselves to anything
God had for us. Ros commented on these times, "They really were
important to me, because it was in this area that we as Christians
knew our work was not 'worldly' in terms of strained relationships,
tiredness, pride in gifts, competition. All these things were offered
sincerely to the Lord and I believe he honoured it and cleansed
us and our motives, allowing the Holy Spirit freedom to touch us
and others as he would."

In the group we often studied the Bible together, especially those narratives or passages we were wanting to interpret through movement. (See chapter 4 for an example of group Bible study which then leads on to a dramatised interpretation.) As with prayer, avoid skimping this or feeling it is not really part of the work in hand. A thorough understanding of a Bible story is vital to its dramatisation. There are bound to come times when the group feels dry in what it is doing, perhaps dispirited or lacking in new ideas. This should be dealt with at two levels—firstly the devotional, and secondly the technical. Plan a day or weekend off together for Bible study, prayer and discussion. Review the whole life and vision of the group and see if God is saying something to you. We had a day retreat at a nearby convent, where we could be undistracted and peaceful, and it turned out to be an important and renewing time. On the technical front, Andy Kelso advises, "revitalise yourselves in improvisational work, in scenes from other plays, in spontaneous work on a psalm or a parable. And revert to technique again!"[1] And, continue to let all the work together be in a context of prayer and God's truth.

(b) *Commitment to the work*

It is all too easy for some of us to take on too many activities, begin to wish we hadn't, then begin opting out. Perhaps the good intention was there and the initial enthusiasm, but somehow we "didn't realise how much it would involve". We are each responsible for what we do and how we use our time and a different set of priorities will emerge for almost every individual. It is as well to warn people who are keen to get involved in a Christian dance-drama group that it will mean a real commitment in terms of time and hard work. Jane Winearls, dancer and lecturer, writing about dance in the church, says: "If there is a case for lay dancers . . . and I think there may be . . . they must be especially prepared and practised, as is the choir. The work must be taken seriously as a job, and the dancers must have a certain level of aptitude and skill. It is not enough to indulge in using dancing to let off steam, however gentle and pleasant the process may seem to be . . . If you want to share, communicate, show others what you know and believe in yourself, work and prepare yourself to improve your talent, for talent it must be, so that you can put that talent to work like a good servant."[2]

So discipline is involved, both for the individual and for the whole group. Rehearsals are a 'must' and if some people are spasmodic in their attendance, it will affect everyone. It is helpful if rehearsal times and dates can be worked out well in advance and, if extra time is needed leading up to a special service or performance, this should be noted by everyone. Try to start punctually and finish at an agreed time then, on those occasions when it seems essential to rehearse overtime, it will be more acceptable if it is unusual rather than the norm. When folk arrive for rehearsal, it is useful to have some time for general conversation and catching up on each other's news before prayer and work begin. We found that if this was built into the pattern for the evening it was better than not allowing for it yet finding that there was chatter during the work time. When work is in progress it is important to be disciplined and cut out unnecessary chatter. This also should apply to those sitting around who might not be involved in the rehearsing of one particular scene or dance whilst others are.

The different kinds of work which emerge in this sort of group are varied and not always obvious at first. Some contributions, such as a solo dance or major acting role, might appear more 'important', yet in the end it is the co-operative creativity and functioning of the whole group that will count. Each person needs to be faithful to his or her particular part whether this is turning knobs, reading a poem, performing a solo dance—or making the coffee! From time to time people will forget or jobs will be skimped—then a reminder about being committed to the work in hand might be timely. Also people learn in different ways and at different rates. Some pick up new ideas or sequences of movement quickly, others less so. We often found it helpful to ask more gifted dancers to use odd times, however short, to coach those who were finding difficulties with certain steps. It was interesting to see how teaching gifts increased amongst them. Gifts of judgment also grew as the group were often asked to sift and evaluate ideas or parts of scripts. This is generally the prerogative of the producer but there is no reason why group members cannot help here too—indeed, their ideas are often valid and even better than his. If the group is committed to work together, the co-operative functioning can result in something far richer, but if each is contributing only in an individualistic way, it will become divisive and impoverished.

Like any other piece of worthwhile work this is sometimes demanding and tiring. Yet there are corresponding rewards and compensations. Wendy, a young teacher, wrote about the dance-drama group: "I was often physically tired after a day at school, a long journey back and a late night. Yet I was also spiritually and mentally refreshed so I went into school the next day feeling more able." If our work is for God and his glory, then standards can afford to be high and nothing too much trouble if the end of it is going to communicate well and memorably. So being committed to the hard work and discipline will be a vital, though not necessarily obtrusive, factor.

(c) *Commitment to each other*

In 1 Corinthians 12:12–26 St. Paul likens the Christian group to a physical body. The body is made up of different limbs and parts, each of which is differently shaped to serve a different function. The ear looks different from the eye, serves a different purpose, yet belongs to the same body. Each part is so linked together that there results a close interrelationship and inter-dependence. A Christian group or fellowship is to discover a similar pattern, with individuals functioning in particular ways which, at the same time, fit together and complement each other. In v. 25 Paul writes of there being "no discord in the body, but that the members may have the same care for one another". So, when a Christian group is working together, a unity and harmony will only become apparent when each person is functioning well as an individual, using his gifts and talents, yet also letting his individuality find its proper place in the whole pattern of the group. This will involve both an appreciation of one's own gifts and, at the same time, a glad acknowledgment of others with their gifts, without which one's own would have no context.

Seen in this light, the quality of relationships within the group is very important and can affect the creativity and work for better or worse. To the extent that there is really mutual care and encouragement, channels remain open for the truth and life of God to be communicated. This kind of group sharing is possible at all kinds of levels and the leader should both model attitudes of encouragement himself and also teach people to help and encourage each other in as many ways as possible. We found that this sort of thing gradually increased—one helping another with a dance routine or group scene, someone else offering to hear the memory work or reading of one of the narrators, offers of transport, repairing the men's clothing and even, when someone complained of frozen feet one winter rehearsal, a sympathetic friend obligingly wrapping her shawl around them! This might seem rather obvious but the consequences of such mutuality are important and will gradually strengthen the group in becoming united in love.

Andrew wrote of what this kind of sharing meant to him: "The fellowship was 'real'. By that I mean there were people who were complete opposites from me but because we were so close and each person had a role—not only acting or singing or dancing but also in the group itself—I came to tolerate and even love people who would normally have rubbed me up the wrong way. I also felt this warmth myself from people I obviously annoyed, which was a precious experience." Of course, relationships will not always come easily. Particularly when working under pressure, they will need to be worked at with determination, honesty, trust and humour. Andy Kelso writes: "Sometimes you will come along to rehearse and feel resentful or tired out, irritated and a thousand and one other things . . . What then is needed is sensitivity one to the other and an awareness that this work of God's is greater than your particular feelings. That does not mean that your feelings are not important! They are, and they must be made known . . . at the very beginning of the rehearsal time, so that there is time to talk and pray things through. If you are not willing to be open and honest when it matters, then you cannot expect freedom and unity in the work together."[3]

Any Christian group, whatever its specific activity and functioning, should be a place of personal and corporate growth where more can be learnt about living together. One student, Janice, who joined our group said: "I had only just become a Christian and being with the group taught me a great deal about Christianity when I knew very little about it. I didn't feel any different in myself but a Christian friend could see the difference and said that she could see I had grown a lot in the Christian life—which, I think, is mainly due to the group." Where there is genuine growth, this will also flow out in love and care for others in and outside the group, including those who criticise the work or are even antagonistic towards such things happening in church buildings.

Also out of this individual and group growth, gifts will emerge that will complement each other so that, instead of people competing against each other or striving after the 'best' parts, there can come a harmonising. In our group we had a talented singer who was more used to solo work than group work when she joined us. Anne wrote: "Whereas at folk clubs or churches to which I was invited I was almost a 'one man show', with Charis (our dance-drama group) I really had to make myself understand that I wasn't just an individual but part of the group and also part of the body of Christ. A group of individuals can only be a team when they swallow enough pride to let themselves become *part* of a team. That was something I had to think out with my head long before my emotions could accept it." This person knew her gift but had to learn new ways of using it. Others might be less sure of what they have to offer and the encouragement and confidence they can begin to experience in a caring group working to certain goals can be, for them, a place where they discover unexplored or even unknown gifts and potentials.

Janice, with no prior training, was asked to learn to operate the tape recorder and discover about P.A. systems. She soon became competent and reliable and saw this as a real answer to prayer. By the time a performance actually began, most of her nervousness had worn off—and nothing ever went wrong! Ros often sang with the group and was also a painter. Sometimes she sat sketching during a dance or piece of dramatic movement and eventually produced two fine paintings of Jesus healing the lepers and forgiving the adulterous woman, which were warmly commended by her tutor for their quality of movement. She said: "I 'knew' that if God was Creator then I should be creating through him, but it wasn't until Charis and the time I spent watching the dance and meditating on the Bible that I was truly inspired and asked God to help me be creative—then I found the freedom I knew existed!" Anne had already studied movement and dance before she joined the group and found that, along with her love of dance, there also emerged an interest in writing. "In dance I found a creative gift which I had longed for, but I also discovered an interest in writing verse and prose. I think far more people are creative than realise it and that it is only when one starts experimenting with communication that one realises that it *is* possible." Two of her poems and a short story have since been published. Sylvia felt that one of her contributions was prayer and she often turned her concern for others into prayer for them. Another member of the group found that her talents lay more in the direction of administration than dancing—it was a great asset to have that kind of help when it came to programme planning, duplicating and other skills.

So, in these and other ways, a group of people can give themselves and their talents to enrich the whole life and output of the ministry. In working together in a caring group, gifts can grow, flourish, be channelled and refined in such ways that the outcome can glorify the Creator and communicate effectively to others.

4. MEDIUM AND MESSAGE

Finally in this chapter it is worth re-emphasising that in sharing truths about God and his Word through dance and drama, there must be a close correspondence between medium and message. The one must befit the other if it is not to deny and invalidate it. It is possible for a group to become technically outstanding yet for their performance to lack soul and their message to lack meaning. I am in no way decrying the value of technique and hard practice, yet there is obviously more to it than that. As well as working out the principle of dramatic identification by exploring character study, stimulating the imagination, extending dramatic vocabulary and understanding the humanity of themselves and others, Christians must also allow themselves to be affected and changed by the very truths they are communicating. Our limbs, faces, minds, spirits, emotions, voices, relationships—in fact, every part of ourselves which we are using to communicate, must be given to God and open to changes which he might choose to effect. In this way the medium will not be estranged from the message but will become part of it. Then, as we become vehicles of God's truth, his Spirit will have increasing space to work both in and through us.

St. Paul teaches that, as Christians, we are "God's temple"—

a holy dwelling place—which God's Spirit inhabits. Exactly how we give the Holy Spirit house-room is both our responsibility and privilege to work out. The principle abides though the activity and context may be different each day. Therefore, whether singing hymns in church or kneeling to pray or dancing in praise or acting a part, we continue to be "temples of the Holy Spirit". This can raise problems in acting some character parts, such as Judas or the adulterous woman or Satan himself. It is possible to over-identify in such a way that a right and proper contact with objectivity is lost. Whatever part a person is acting he must not only have thought-through the character identification in detail, but must also retain some control of it. If there is going to be a high degree of involvement, there must still remain some degree of objectivity. This is particularly important in the portrayal of evil.

I was especially impressed by the way this principle of identi-fication was handled by the Mary Sisters of Darmstadt, West Germany. They are an evangelical community with a wide Chris-tian ministry and outreach. Occasionally they perform "Herald plays" to which many visitors come to make up a very large audience. I read through an English translation of the German script beforehand and was very unimpressed by what struck me as the stylised and wooden dialogue of their version of the parable of the wise and foolish virgins. Yet the performance turned out to be memorable for two reasons. Firstly, the message of the parable came over loud and clear that, since we do not know the timing of Christ's return, we are at all times to be prepared. Secondly, there was a radiance about the wise virgins and a pathos about the foolish ones which was very striking and underlined the whole message. The audience was deeply moved, some to tears, as God's Word communicated powerfully and truthfully. I dis-covered afterwards that the Herald plays are considered a sig-nificant part of the Community's evangelistic outreach and that those taking part in the acting or singing prepare themselves for some hours before each presentation through prayer, fasting and meditation on the Scriptures. Those taking the part of the foolish, unprepared virgins identified, in this preparation, with those in the world who have no time for God, sorrowing with and for them and praying for them. The results of their work certainly showed a very close integration of medium and message which has stayed with me ever since.

There is no doubt that, as we learn to work together with love and integrity, hard work and single-mindedness, God will communicate his truth through us. There will be important learning amongst those taking part and learning too amongst those who watch. At a weekend workshop we spent part of the time thinking about and dramatising how the sin of humanity had resulted in Christ's death. One young man wrote afterwards: "It enabled me to appreciate for the first time on an emotional level the meaning of Christ's death on the cross. Until now I have known and appreciated the fact on an intellectual basis but not emotionally. So for me this is a real step forward and something I have been praying about for some time." Many people who watched different dramatisations also wrote telling us of fresh insights gained which caused them to worship God or take steps forward in their own lives.

As a Christian dance-drama group sorts out its priorities and works out its commitment, so there will be a good and exciting outcome.

CHAPTER 3

Getting a Group Moving

1. MOVEMENT VOCABULARY

JUST AS VERBAL communication (e.g. a shared conversation, a speech, giving an instruction, an explanation) means that we must first have learnt words, phrases, sentence construction, grammar, expression and fluency, so it must be with communication which involves our bodies. If bodily movements and gestures are to say something that will communicate with integrity, there must be a learning of physical language and vocabulary. It might be fun to wave an arm or kick a leg, but what is it saying? The more parts of our person we use to make or communicate an expression, the more connections there must be between those different parts of the body, mind and emotions. Professional dancers spend hour after hour in practising and disciplining their bodies in order to extend and refine their movement vocabulary. Violet Bruce and Joan Tooke write in *Lord of the Dance*, "Dance uses the normal possibilities of human movement but exploits and perfects them so that its language is capable of expressing and communicating what the dancer wishes to 'say' with clarity and fullness of meaning. A dancer expresses not with outside media which he handles and moulds, as with paint and clay, but with himself. . . . So it is necessary to investigate the language of movement with which one needs to be familiar."[1]

Amateurs who are most likely to be involved in the kind of groups this book is written for, need to be ready for much hard work, discipline—and stiff muscles! Of course there is a great deal of enjoyment and fun, but, especially where a group is preparing something which will then be received and shared by others, the disciplined practising and limbering are essential. With our own group (most of whom were learning some movement and dance as part of their training for teaching children), there was already some basic understanding of modern dance. Even so, we found it helpful to 'import' a specialist in movement from time to time. In some churches there may well be a trained teacher who can give this kind of help, especially if the group wants to move ahead and present public performances. But if this is not possible, it does not necessarily mean that a group cannot function. For keen leaders there are helpful books (see Bibliography), local and national courses, and an increasing number of Christian workshops and groups. A clear analysis of movement can be found in chapter 4 of *Creative Dance in the Secondary School* by Joan Russell. Her *Modern Dance in Education*, though earlier, is still very useful. If simple categories are wanted, chapter 2 of *Lord of the Dance* by Violet Bruce and Joan Tooke is helpful and straightforward. Very many teachers, especially in primary schools, are used to teaching children in this way, and have learnt these methods as part of their own training.

2. Some Barriers to Overcome

I hope, with these simple comments, to have established the point that in creating dance dramas, there must be a proper inclusion of basic bodily movement training and the oiling of creaking bones which will help the participants to gain confidence, and extend their capabilities and range of expression. But in doing this, there will be certain barriers to work through, for which the leader must be prepared. To start with, and especially with a new group of adults, there may well be embarrassment, apparent in giggling, laughter, and sometimes a lack of ease about getting into the work. They are about to join in an unusual activity, which involves them in using their bodies in a self-conscious way, and some will find this difficult. I have found, especially with many clergy and those whose education has been concentrated upon the mind and cerebral activity, that there is often an initial reluctance to 'speak' with the body instead of using words. For some, it will be fun and releasing really to get back into their bodies, but not for all; the leader needs to understand this and expect a very varied response from a group.

Linked with embarrassment, some may feel initially nervous about being watched. After all, our bodies are an important part of our person, and supposing, by attempting this kind of work, we are laughed at or criticised? In the early stages of group work, I make a point of working towards an atmosphere of enjoyment and fun without laughing *at* individuals, and also giving a great deal of individual and group encouragement. There will be time later for criticism and working at weaknesses. I also ask as a group starts working together that everyone should join in so that no one apart from myself is observing. Later on, those moving will mind far less about having each other as spectators and critics, but this should be reserved for a stage when defences are not so important, and people can afford to become far more self-critical.

The leader may also encounter anxiety if someone feels they cannot do what is being asked of them. Clear instruction, encouragement, and some individual help may well overcome the anxiety. Most people have far greater powers of self-expression in their bodies than they realise, or have ever attempted. If I am about to work with an unknown group (e.g. a weekend workshop) I previously pray about my initial rapport with them, for it is in the early stages of our work together that people can begin to feel an exciting potential—both within themselves and in the group project—and a growth of freedom and sharing. A skilful leader will prepare carefully towards making the group a real fellowship group where gifts can emerge. (If the group are meeting each other as well as you for the first time, be prepared to spend some time in leisurely introductions and getting to know each other.) It is also best if people have been previously asked to come suitably dressed in trousers or leotards (rather than skirts), comfortable sweaters or tops which are loose and not restrictive. Preferably, feet should be bare, depending on the condition of the floor. If possible, work in a large space where people have enough room to lie flat on the floor, run and jump and feel reasonably free. Have a record player or tape recorder available and a drum for beating out rhythms.

3. STARTING OFF

If I were meeting a group for the first time, I would spend some time in establishing an easy relationship with them through mutual introductions and a clarifying of the group task. Perhaps a weekend workshop has met together to prepare a piece of drama for the Sunday evening service or for some future occasion. Certainly, if this is a newly-formed group, it will be helpful to discuss in a preliminary way goals and expectations. Tactfully discover any injuries or strains people may have suffered in the past and urge them to take care. Knee trouble will generally mean no kneeling, stomach or back trouble not too much stretching, etc. This may seem obvious but is a necessary and simple precaution for both leader and group members. If it is a previously-established group, then it is best to get some movement and limbering as soon as possible, though do not overlook the value of mutual greeting and meeting first.

I approach the limbering work in two sections, first concentrating on how the body and its various parts move, and secondly how it can, through movement and mime, interpret and 'say' things. So we have a section of movement exercises and then one of improvisation. I would introduce any rehearsal with some limbering-up including these two elements. If it were right at the beginning of a group, I would go into this by demonstrating myself some simple body movements—a sudden, quick arm movement, compared with a slow, smooth, flowing one; or a strong, tense stamp of the leg and foot as compared with a small, light flick of the toes. Different parts of the body can move in different ways, at different speeds, at different levels, and using the space differently. They can say a whole variety of things—and I suggest simple phrases, such as "I'm listening", "I'm curious", "I'm afraid", "I'm superior", "I'm angry", etc., and demonstrate equivalent body movements, the sort we often use in everyday life. I also demonstrate a few simple movements in the area of relationships, such as "I welcome you", "I have something tiny to show you", "I'm annoyed with you". Every day we use our bodies to communicate and often to underline or clarify our speech. Our heads and necks can be erect and proud, bowed in shame, hunched into our shoulders. With our arms and hands we can express so many things—joy, outgoing welcome, criticism, rigidity, health—and our legs and feet also can run and jump, bend and kneel, stretch and curl. Our bodies can be tense and alert, sagging and listless. The eyes and their direction are a powerful means of communicating a whole range of messages— anxiety, peace, fear, terror, happiness, suspicion, excitement. Think, too, of what different messages can be communicated by bodily stillness, either tense or relaxed.

At this initial stage, it can be fun to demonstrate a piece of non-verbal communication to show just how well the body can speak for itself (e.g. I am asleep, the alarm clock rings, I turn it off, turn over and go back to sleep, I suddenly awake, look at the clock, jump out of bed, dress, clean my teeth and brush my hair, run downstairs, trip over the cat, leave the house, go to the underground station, 'strap-hang' to work, yawning frequently, arrive at the office, sit at a typewriter and type, etc., etc.). Or you might discuss how you can often partly tell how a person is feeling from the way he is sitting. Some psychiatrists and therapists set considerable store by 'body language' and the abilities of the body to communicate very effectively what is in the mind and emotions. Or have a guessing game, mirroring a few different actions and asking people to guess what you are doing—eating spaghetti, walking over a stream on stepping stones, having a golf lesson, playing a piano scale, etc. By all means, introduce an element of fun to help the group relax and yet also to see the point you are making—that our bodies can speak. And now it is time for the group themselves to get moving.

4. Body Exercises

A variety of these exercises should be chosen for a limbering session. In the early stages it is useful to remember four things: do not overtax the muscles too much at first; choose a variety of exercises that will bring movement to each area of the body rather than one part only; use rhythm, where possible keeping to one rhythm for each exercise; and do not go on for too long without a break. With a new group, I would attempt about half-an-hour of dramatic improvisation followed by discussion and sharing. At a later stage, and when actually working towards some dance or drama, reduce the amount of time given to warming up and get on with the project. But remember that some initial warming-up is always necessary especially in a poorly-heated hall and with people who have been sitting down all day.

Choose a few exercises only from each section below. Do not attempt to cover them all.

(a) Relaxation and breathing

(i) Lie flat on the back with arms stretched out on the ground behind the head. Stretch out with the toes and fingers, giving tension and tone to the body right through, breathing in, and 'grow'; hold, then relax, breathing out. This should first be done in the person's own time, then the leader should talk through each part of the body which is stretching and relaxing (toes, feet and ankles, calves, thighs, hips, chest, shoulders, neck, head, arms, hands and fingers). Repeat exercise two or three times.

(ii) Lie flat on the back with arms by each side. Wiggle each part of the body in turn, from the toes up. Lift each leg to wiggle it, each arm, each hand, the shoulders, the head. Relax. There will probably be some cracking joints at this stage!

(iii) Lie flat on the back and tense different parts in turn, then relax them (e.g. tense and clench the fists then relax them; tense and screw up the feet then relax them; tense the arms and shoulders then relax them; tense and screw up the face then relax it; etc.). I normally walk around amongst them as they are lying on the floor, talking through instructions and encouraging their efforts.

(iv) Still on the back, with arms stretched out behind the head, breathe in through the nose to eight (claps or drum beats), stretching the body, hold the breath, then slowly and at one's own rate, exhale through the mouth, letting the muscles and arms relax. Repeat two or three times.

(v) Lie in a similar position, but this time place the hands lightly across the rib cage, with middle fingers just touching. Breathe in to four, hold—feeling how the rib cage has expanded and the fingers parted—then exhale through the mouth, so that the fingers move together again. Repeat two or three times. Try to expand sideways rather than forward.

(vi) Sit cross-legged with the arms stretched out on either side and the fingers lightly touching the floor. Breathe in to four, slowly raising the arms like wings. Hold the breath and arms still, then exhale through the mouth to four, slowly lowering the arms. Keep the head and neck up and avoid heaving the shoulders up. The expansion is sideways in the rib cage.

At this stage, I usually ask them to listen to themselves breathing and become conscious of the air being inhaled and exhaled. We never stop breathing day and night, but we rarely pause to consider the wonder of it. Very often we allow our breathing to become superficial whilst our bodies become tense and tired. Most of us would do well to give more thought to the quality of our breathing.

(vii) Before standing up, curl up small on the floor, then, to eight beats, slowly stretch the limbs in any direction, breathing in. Hold the position, then to a rapid drum patter, curl up quickly again into a ball, breathing out. Repeat, finding a different extended position this time. Sense the contrasting feelings of being curled up and closed and being stretched and open. Try to 'open' the body and face as well as the limbs. This exercise is quite strenuous on the stomach muscles, therefore do not repeat it more than three times and use breath to assist dynamics.

(b) *Body movement* ✤

(i) Standing with feet slightly apart and knees straight, flop down from the hips, then slowly uncurl upwards like a poster being pasted on a board, to eight beats. Use the stomach muscles rather than the shoulders to pull the body up and bring the head up last of all. Now flop down again from the waist. This exercise can be done to four/four music (i.e. for *two* bars of music, begin down, four beats to uncurl, flop down on five, keeping hanging down for six, seven, eight. For *three* bars, use eight beats to uncurl, flop down on nine, keep hanging down for ten, eleven, twelve).

(ii) Standing with feet together, swing arms backwards and forwards bending at the knees and waist in a ski-ing movement.

Continue, carefully keeping the balance. Relax neck on backwards swing, so head hangs forward and upper spine curves forward. In between, stretch arms straight up, straighten knees and back. (Warning: the muscles behind the knees and in the calves will soon ache with this one!)

(iii) Standing with feet together and knees straight, bounce the palms of the hands on the floor in front seven times, keeping stomach pulled up, and on the eighth beat straighten up into a standing position. (If it is not possible to touch the floor, do not over-strain but get down as far as possible.) Then, from the upright position, stretch over the left side bouncing to seven beats and up on the eighth. Do not lean forward but simply stretch the muscles in the side. Now do the same stretching over the right side to seven beats and up on the eighth. Complete the exercise by stretching backwards from the waist to seven beats and up on the eighth. If very stiff, allow the knees to bend slightly. Never bend backwards thinking of the waist but, stretching the waist, lead back with the top of the head to curve the upper spine followed by the waist area. This exercise can also be done to four/four music.

(iv) Make as many angular, pointed movements as you can with different parts of the body—spiked fingers and hands, jutting chin, hips, knees, heels and toes. Move around the room making these angular movements.

(v) Choose a word, e.g. 'freedom', and spell it out with different parts of the body—an arm movement for one letter, a leg movement or head movement for another, a rotating of the hips for another.

(c) *Weight transference*

(i) Stand with feet together and legs straight, body stretched to its full height, head erect. Gradually lean the weight forward as far as you can without falling, or moving the feet, then return to the upright position. Repeat this to the right and left and backwards, returning to centre between each and 'feeling' the shift of the weight in each direction. Also note the automatic body mechanism of self-preservation that comes into play instantly if you go a fraction too far. The body will save itself and not allow you to fall, by transferring the weight to one foot in the direction of the fall and spreading the basis of balance. (This exercise is usually done in the dancer's own timing so that it is not hurried and the change of weight is really felt.)

(ii) Stand with the legs apart and hands on the hips. Now take a long step forward, following through the weight with the whole body. Now take another step, transferring the weight in that direction. Move slowly around the floor in this way.

(iii) Lie down on the back, then, finding different body positions, support yourself on different points of the body (e.g. on a hip and an elbow, or stretched out sideways and supported on an extended leg and hand, lying on the back and moving the legs up into the air to balance on the shoulders, supporting the body on an elbow and a knee, etc.).

(iv) Take a strong piece of elastic about one and a half metres long, twist an end around each hand to hold it securely and experiment with different body shapes (e.g. put the elastic round a foot or even one toe and stretch the leg, or the arms. Try crossing your arms or lying down to stretch the elastic with your feet. Some interesting shapes will emerge.)

(v) In a rather similar way, two, three or four people can experiment with a circle of wide, strong elastic, one getting inside it and leaning on it, another pulling it and stretching, or two people experimenting with weight transference with the elastic.

(d) Footwork

(i) Standing with legs slightly apart, slowly rise up on to the toes to four beats, then down to four beats, trying not to sway back too far on heels. This needs concentration to maintain the balance. Repeat several times. Intersperse with knee bends (heels on floor) to relax backs of legs.

(ii) Standing with the legs apart, jump from one foot to the other sideways, straightening the foot and leg in between, and landing on a flexed leg.

(iii) Running on the spot, keep the feet stretched with toes straight and pointed. Gradually lift the knees and feet higher until level with the waist, then gradually lower them again until they hardly come up from the floor. Really stretch the foot muscles, calves and upper legs in this exercise.

(iv) Walk four steps, pause and do two kicks, one foot to the left and the other to the right. Walk another four steps, pause and stamp twice, once with each foot. Walk another four steps, pause and point with a heel, then with a toe. Other variations can be added, using the feet in different ways. Use four/four music.

(e) *Arms and hands*

(i) With the arms and hands, describe different size circles in the air at different levels, using smooth, flowing movements. Use first one arm then the other, then both together. Make a tiny circle with one finger, or another with an elbow or another with a shoulder. Make a sideways circle or draw some on the ground.

(ii) In a similar way, write your own name in the air using arm, hand and finger movements. Use a background of quiet music if you wish. Let your movements flow.

(iii) Now with the arms, hands and fingers draw angular shapes, triangles or squares. Vary the size of these, and the levels. You might stand for some, kneel for others, lie down for others.

(iv) Trace imaginary patterns or shapes of objects in the air at different speeds, sometimes letting the hand travel slowly and sometimes quickly, sometimes lingering and sometimes darting.

(v) In a similar way, and with a chiffon scarf tied around one wrist, make patterns in the air, whipping, fluttering, high, low, smooth, jagged. Now take the scarf off, throw it and catch it at different levels and in different ways.

(f) *Locomotion and group work*

(i) Walk round the room at different levels, first eight steps crouched down with knees bent, then eight at normal height, then eight steps walking on the toes, then eight on the toes with arms stretched high in the air.

(ii) Run across the floor slowly as a group (divide the group into two if there is insufficient space), with legs stretched and bodies as erect as possible.

(iii) Run across the floor as a group and, on a single drum beat or cymbal clash, jump high into the air.

(iv) Run across the floor as a group and, on the drum beat, stop dead. This requires real body and muscle control—some professionals find it difficult. Therefore, don't be surprised if you over-balance!

(v) With hands on hips, take four long strides, stretching each side of the body as you do so. Then do a few small running steps. Repeat the long strides and intersperse with running steps. Do this in your own time without keeping time with the rest of the group.

(vi) Walk across the floor seven steps and on the eighth jump and turn direction, pointing the toes. Again, take seven steps and on the eighth jump and turn direction. Four/four music can be used.

(vii) For those who are preparing to present drama on a stage or in public in any given space, it may be useful to increase awareness of orientation and direction by working to precise patterns sometimes. Imagine a square drawn round the performer on the floor and turn to face the front of the square, the back, each side in turn, each corner in turn. Move forward, backward and sideways facing these various directions, thus using diagonal moves across the space given, straight crossing moves and patterns involving both. Progress to circles (facing centre of circle, backing centre, facing along circumference, sideways travelling along the circle, going into the centre on one tangent and out on another, joining two circles together and walking a figure of eight, etc.).

This gives an awareness of floor-pattern which is useful in movement sequences, and will also involve a knowledge of what the audience can see, how the angle of a movement makes it more or less clear to the onlooker. It will increase the clarity of purpose behind the moves later decided upon and help to make movements repeatable without a random change of placing in the group and its members causing confusion.

(viii) Awareness of space and of group interaction may also be explored in exercises where the whole group has to share a space whilst each member is moving at a different pace and improvising his movements. Dancers must avoid colliding but not compromise their movements too much, e.g. one who has chosen hopping movements must continue to hop when meeting another dancer choosing to roll along the floor—the hopper has either to hop over or round or ahead of the roller! If two dancers suddenly meet easily in the dance a reaction may be appropriate; it must fit in with the type of movement each is doing, but could undergo a transformation when the two dance together, or acknowledge each other before passing on.

After using a variety of these exercises from the different sections to flex different parts of the body, have a short rest and discover how people are feeling. Then continue with some improvisation exercises chosen from the following. Many other ideas are to be found in different books on improvisation. There is, for example, a wide selection in Brian Way's *Development through Drama*.

5. IMPROVISATION

These suggestions introduce a more imaginative quality of movement. They both build on the previous section, in that different parts of the body are used, and also offer the mind and imagination plenty of ideas to interpret. To encourage confidence, I usually start by letting individuals work alone, then in pairs, then in small groups and finally in one large group. Choose a variety of the following ideas for the improvisation section of your warming-up.

(a) *Individual interpretation*

(i) Describe with your bodies the following: "I'm listening", "I'm frightened", "I'm self-protective", "I'm angry", "I'm delighted", "I'm imploring", "I worship", "I retreat", "I'm puzzled", etc. Explain how, with our differing personalities, we will express emotions in different ways. What feels genuine to us? Do we tend to use our bodies much in self-expression or concentrate more upon words? The aim here is to find movement that feels right for each of us, rather than standardised gestures or steps.

(ii) You are cautiously walking across a stream on stepping stones, using your hands and arms to balance your body. You will need concentration and balance for this. (The leader might keep up a commentary about the stream, the shape and texture of the stones, the weeds, etc., to help people exercise their imagination.)

(iii) You are on a country walk and suddenly a storm breaks. Dart from tree to tree for cover and shelter until the storm subsides. (Again, the leader should keep up a descriptive commentary and use a drum or cymbals for thunder effects.)

(iv) You are cramped up in an imaginary box so that you cannot stand upright. It is dark inside and you cannot see. Feel all around your box, its shape, its texture, its size and decide whether to try to get out of it or whether to remain inside.

(v) You are bound up in sticky twine which is restricting and cramping your body, arms, legs and head. You start trying to remove the twine and discover it to be far more difficult than you imagined. You will need to experiment with many different body shapes of bending and stretching until you finally remove it.

(vi) You bend down to stroke and play with a kitten. Feel the texture of its fur, look at its paws, ears, tail, tickle its stomach, play with it, pick it up. Spend a few minutes on the floor with your kitten.

(vii) You are alone in a long, dark, underground tunnel. If you remain there, you may not be discovered, so you tentatively start travelling, using your hands and feet to test out the path and tunnel walls, neither of which you can see. Perhaps it is not tall enough for you to stand upright, perhaps in places it is very narrow, or wet and squishy underfoot. After a few minutes you dimly see a speck of light far ahead and, with renewed hope, decide to press on even though it involves such effort. At some stage you will need to clamber upwards and, at last, you are in the light, safe and able to stretch your limbs. (Suitable music or a muffled drum beat might be used to help the imagination.) Afterwards you could all sit down for a short break and discuss how it felt in the tunnel and whether it was an exciting or unpleasant experience.

(viii) Crouch or lie on the floor and be a fire. Start with a tiny, flickering flame from one part of your body and let the flame grow up, gradually affecting other parts of you. Explore the surrounding space and gradually rise up until your whole body is part of the moving flame. Then let the flame die down again until it is a still, smouldering ember. (A variation could include a moving around to unite with other flames, interrelating flickering hands, fingers, arms, whirling bodies, darting forward and back as the fire grows and burns.)

(ix) Think of something you would very much like to have. Take time to decide what it is before you go further. This thing is near at hand and you can move towards it. Show with your body the attraction of the thing and make movements towards it. As you get close, take time to examine it closely, look all around it, feel and appreciate it, smell it, taste it, show your enjoyment. Then gradually move away from it, still feeling its attraction.

You could improvise a similar sequence about something undesirable or frightening and note the different quality of movements and different feelings involved.

(x) All stand in a large circle. Moving round clockwise, improvise the following in turn: walking home in new shoes that are too tight; feeling stiff in all your muscles as you walk back from the drama class; an elderly person suffering from rheumatism walking in the park; a blind person needing to use his hands to help him along; you stub your toes, wince and hop, etc. In this exercise, people in the circle do not relate to each other, but concentrate on their own actions. Walking in the same direction helps to prevent traffic jams!

(xi) Select one natural object from a collection in the middle of the group (e.g. different shaped stones, pieces of wood, shells, leaves, twigs, etc.). Take time to examine your object in detail— its colour, shape, contours, feel, smell. Look at it from different angles. Now identify with your object or some part of it, and move into a position which feels like that which you have seen and experienced. Afterwards, share with someone nearby what this exercise was like for you.

(b) *Work in pairs*

As people begin to get used to working as individuals, so they will be more ready and less embarrassed to join with others to work out movements together.

(i) Take a partner and stand facing each other. One of you, using your right hand, flat palm uppermost, will 'paint' on a glass panel which stands between you, using different quality movements, high and low, quick and slow, straight and curved, smooth and zig-zag. The other person, standing opposite and using his left hand, will keep watching his partner and, without letting hands touch, will follow each movement with his hand, as though painting on the other side of the glass. This calls for concentration and careful watching and following. Keep changing roles as to which partner leads and which follows. With practice two can work together so that there is no leader but a close oneness as each is open to the other.

(ii) In twos again, sit down; one person is to decide on an activity, which he will teach his partner (e.g. how to knit, how to make an omelette, how to bed a plant, etc.). Talk about the task first and work out appropriate movements together, including matching facial expressions, then mime it. Having worked it out, couples could show other pairs their tasks and let them guess what is happening. This can both be fun and also allow for a gradual growth in awareness of others and their movements, which, at this stage, will not be too serious or critical.

(iii) Work out a difference of opinion which leads to an argument, heated feelings and cold war. Then decide on how to effect a reconciliation. Use words to work it out then, having decided on the sequence, mime it.

I often pause after an exercise like this and talk about the different ways we react when caught up in argument and division. How can we differ without becoming divisive? How does division affect our thinking, our feeling and our behaviour towards each other? What does reconciliation involve?

(iv) For this exercise, divide the group into two. One half are to be objects which are incomplete (e.g. a chair, a necklace, a

statue, etc.). The other half are to meet up with them and complete them. Couples can talk about what they are and the shapes
involved, then experiment with finding the best way of completing
their shape. This example can also, like the one above, have both
a fun element and a more serious one. In what sense are we, as
individuals, incomplete? Paul talks about the Christian fellowship
as a body in 1 Corinthians chapter 12 whose limbs join together
and work in co-operation. How does this work out amongst ourselves? In what ways do we need each other—even in this working
group? What are some of the difficulties of working together in
close fellowship?

(v) In pairs, work out a battle sequence. The battle might be
between a sick person and death, or good and evil, or war and
peace. Each person should decide which part he is playing, then
a sequence of movements should be worked out. Do not actually
touch or push each other or make any bodily contact, but use
advancing and retreating movements at different levels and with
different body shapes. Let the shapes of the two bodies relate and
interlock without touching. This will need careful working out and
good balance and muscle control. Make it into a sequence of six
or eight advancing and retreating movements and decide which
partner is eventually going to triumph.

(c) *Small group work*

Gradually, as pairs become more used to working together, go
on to small group work in fours or fives.

(i) Work out a still group position to portray mutual care. Take
a few minutes to experiment with different bodily positions. Does
it feel like a pose only? If so, discuss what would feel like a more
caring position for each person. Is the group shape harmonious,
and is each individual a comfortable part of that harmony? When
each group has worked out its best position, show the results, one
group at a time, to the others.

(ii) Try an exercise in rejection-acceptance. One person in each
group becomes the scapegoat and is rejected by the others. This
makes them feel self-righteous, smug and superior. But gradually,

and one at a time, they begin to feel regretful and guilty, realising they have rejected a friend. They decide how to make amends, apologise and welcome him/her back again in order to form a caring group. They will need to discuss how this is to be done, and the rejected person will need to explain to them what gestures of acceptance and welcome feel real or unreal. Afterwards, discuss generally how they felt in doing this. Was it difficult to be rejecting, or quite easy? How did the 'scapegoat' feel? How do we cope in everyday life with rejection? What expressions of acceptance feel to us most meaningful and real? Does this exercise say anything about the ways we treat each other in our church fellowship?

This exercise, and possibly exercise (iii) in the previous section, could cause some of the group, especially if they have problems over rejection or anger, to react deeply, unexpectedly stirring up all sorts of subconscious depths. A leader or producer would only use this type of exercise when he knows the group fairly well, has prayed both for and with them and arrived at an open and sharing relationship.

(iii) Between you, become a machine with interlocking parts. Experiment with different positions to make as interesting a machine as you can. One might stand, one kneel, and one lie down. There might be a wheel turning (hand movement), or a piston shooting in and out (a foot movement). There might be different sounds coming from your machine, and the different parts might interact with different rhythms. But, whatever the parts, the whole machine will work together harmoniously. When you are ready, show the other groups the machine.

(iv) Someone in the group finds a small, interesting object on the ground. He beckons the others across to have a look at it. One by one they take it and examine it carefully. Without using words, they eventually decide what this object is and what they will do with it. (This exercise makes a good opportunity to talk about group sensitivity and working together. The working-out should be discussed but the completed action mimed.)

(v) Work out between you a mimed sequence on birth, growth, maturity, decline and death. This might be treated in human terms or applied to a seed—plant, egg—bird, caterpillar—moth, etc.

(vi) Sit round in small group circles. One by one each person sits in the middle and each person in the circle mimes the giving of a present to the one in the middle. The present is something specially chosen for that particular individual (e.g. a precious jewel, a book, a piece of sports equipment). The giver mimes his gift, then uses words to explain why he has chosen this particular gift for the recipient (e.g. "John, because you enjoy reading so much, I've chosen this very big book of detective stories so that it will last a long time." "Judy, I give you this jewel because when you're enjoying yourself, you really seem to sparkle!")

(vii) As a group, work out a sequence of situation—crisis—resolution, then mime it. (e.g. You are driving along in a car, you suddenly see a fallen tree across the road, you all get out, and, with great difficulty, try to shift it. After much effort, you manage to drag it to one side. You then continue your journey.)

(viii) Discover group positions or movements to portray words like: compassion, sin, worship, mistrust, fellowship, hunger, forgiveness. Avoid quick posing and spend time in discussing what these words mean to each of the group and how a true meaning can be conveyed bodily. Generally, with expressions of need and negative states, the body will be directed downwards and inwards whereas with positive expressions of good, outgoing qualities, the body will be directed upwards and outwards.

(d) *Whole group work*

By now, people should be feeling sufficiently relaxed to work together as a whole group for some exercises of improvisation, just as they will be working together later on in working out a whole dance drama or movement sequence.

(i) It is a sunny, spring day, and you are in a lively town square full of people and interest—mothers with prams and small children, young men passing the time of day, older men sitting watching, shoppers, cyclists, and motorists, a paper vendor, and even a flower girl at her stall. Decide who you will be and how you will follow through your mimed sequence. Now try it through, with some bustling background music. (The probability is that, first time through, the movement will be jumbled and unrelated. Offer some direction—who will stop to greet someone? Who will go shopping? Who will trip over, and who will come to their help? Work out a simple narrative sequence and then try again. Encourage people to be specific in the movements and gestures they are using.)

(ii) You are escaping at night from enemy territory, and you are about to cross no-man's-land. Nearby, the enemy stand guard with machine-guns. Amongst your group are one or two wounded. Start making your way across the room as quietly as possible. Use different levels—walking, creeping, wriggling. When you hear a machine-gun (fast beating drum), freeze until it stops, then continue until you reach the safety zone. Use bodily tension to heighten a sense of drama. (If the floor area is rather small, divide the group into two and work with half at a time. There is no need to act the part of the enemy. Let everyone be in the role of the escapers, and you, as producer, can control the action with a drum and an improvised narrative.)

(iii) Two people sense that something enjoyable is going to happen in the street. They beckon to others, who gradually join them. There is anticipation, curiosity, excitement, craning of necks. Fix *exact* direction for all eyes to look, or succession of points of movement. What is it that is coming down the street? A circus procession! As it draws near, the people cheer, jump up to see better, laugh, point, etc. The procession passes, and after happy banter and talk, the crowd disperses again. (The procession is imagined rather than acted. Those in the crowd need to work out in detail what they see and do. Random jumping and cheering will not be good enough, and, as in exercise (i), clear sequences and relationships need to be talked through and worked out. Cheerful music should be used after movements have been discussed.)

(iv) Work out a movement sequence around a pictorial idea. For example, on the theme of water, start with some people being a meandering stream, then the rain comes (other people) and the stream swells to a fast-moving river. As it flows on, moving round and about, it becomes a flood which eventually rushes out into the sea. You might look together at pictures or slides of water, discussing the different qualities of movement to be used. For sound, you might begin with a triangle, building up with a tambourine, using a drum for the heavy rainfall, and adding music as the flood swirls along. (Such as *Die Moldau*, the orchestral tone poem by Smetana.)

(v) Work out a similar sequence on the theme of wind, starting with a gentle, swaying breeze, then letting it grow into a strong wind, then a boisterous gale, then gradually dying down again. For extra effect, tie a chiffon scarf to a wrist and use it for waving and whisking during the dance.

(vi) Starting off in one large circle, weave an imaginary tapestry, individuals moving one by one across the central space to change places with others opposite them, each holding an imaginary thread. Twist and turn, be sensitive to how and where others are moving. Imagine that a patterned fabric is emerging in the central space. Move at different speeds and levels, and avoid crashing as you move. At an agreed signal, stop, lift the completed tapestry, each person round the circle holding part of its edge, and together gently set it down and sit on the floor to look at it.

(vii) Quietly move around, meeting each other one at a time and affirming each other by speaking his/her name (e.g. Paul walks to Mary, looks at her, and says her name, "Mary". She repeats her name, whilst looking at him, "Mary". She then says his name, "Paul", and he repeats it, "Paul".). This can be an effective, simple way of meeting and greeting, which draws together the large group. Finish by standing, hand in hand, in one circle and looking round at each other in silence. Or, at this point, a group could pray together.

Just as you can choose a balanced variety of the body exercises, so you can pick out a variety of these improvisation exercises, encouraging people to use as many different parts of their bodies as they can, to express ideas, thoughts and scenes. Be prepared, as the producer, to improvise narratives or descriptions to help them use the imagination. There are very many English words that have a movement quality in them and are a useful stimulus to the imagination. An exercise could be to think of (or look up) as many different words for walking as possible and experiment by putting them into action (e.g. stroll, saunter, pace, march, ramble, tramp, stride, strut, prance, bound, etc.). Such words are evocative and would bring images and memories to mind and discussion. Or write the words on a blackboard, let some of the group act them out whilst others guess which word is being acted. Encourage them in their efforts and, where you see a person whose movement is limited and inhibited, quietly give some individual help and ideas. At some stage during the warming-up, all sit down in groups of three or four, and for five minutes tell each other how you are feeling about what you are doing, and the ways you are using your body to speak and act out ideas. Mutual acceptance and understanding of each other is important, and helps to lay an important foundation for further work together.

CHAPTER 4

The Ten Lepers

So far we have suggested some ideas for beginning dramatic movement, progressing to themes and small scenes. It is now time to outline in some detailed ways and means of dramatising a narrative with a group of people and to look at the different stages involved in the group's work together. These stages might extend over several weeks if the group were meeting once a week or, working in a more concentrated way, it could become one evening's theme (a fairly long evening preferably!) or, interspersed with discussion and other kinds of creativity, a weekend workshop project.

Obviously different Bible narratives may be interpreted in many different ways dramatically, perhaps as a result of scripting or by group discussion and working it out together. Here is a fairly detailed outline of one interpretation of the healing of the ten lepers.

On the way to Jerusalem he was passing along between Samaria and Galilee. And as he entered a village he was met by ten lepers, who stood at a distance and lifted up their voices and said, "Jesus, Master, have mercy on us". When he saw them he said to them, "Go and show yourselves to the priests": And as they went they were cleansed. Then one of them, when he saw that he was healed, turned back, praising God with a loud voice; and he fell on his face at Jesus' feet, giving him thanks. Now he was a Samaritan. Then said Jesus, "Were not ten cleansed? Where are the nine? Was no-one found to return and give praise to God except this foreigner?" And he said to

him, "Rise and go your way; your faith has made you well".
(Luke 17:11–19, R.S.V.)

1. BIBLE STUDY

First, sit down with the group to read and discuss the passage.
It is helpful if each person has a Bible and the leader, or one of
the group, should previously have prepared some facts to share.
Pray together for understanding and insight into the narrative.

Where did this incident take place? What might the countryside
have been like and what might the village setting have been where
the encounter took place? A Bible atlas and pictures will help
here. What sort of problem was leprosy in those days and what
were the religious laws of cleansing which the priests had to
enforce? What social precautions did lepers have to take? What
was the significance of the thankful leper being a Samaritan?

(It might also be noted at this early stage of preparation that
the incident, as it is recorded, has a fine dramatic structure—there
is a clear-cut situation, climax and resolution.)

2. FACTS AND INFORMATION

What does the group already know about leprosy? One or two
people may have been asked to do some fact-finding on the subject. Information and pictures can be procured, or perhaps trans-
parencies borrowed from a missionary. What is the nature of the
disease and its effects upon the body? What about the personal,
psychological and social stigma involved? In which countries is it
found? What kind of preventive medicine is used in leprosy control
today? Who knows of any missionary doctors or nurses involved
in this work? Has anyone read of the surgical developments made
by Dr. Paul Brand, a medical missionary? Plenty of discussion,
looking at pictures and sharing facts will inform the mind and
imagination.

3. Preliminary Movement

After initial study, now try some preliminary movements, using descriptive words and phrases to stir the imagination. Gradually talk the group into the part they are playing. "Find a twisted shape. Some of you may have fingers or toes missing, a disfigured face, a bent body, gnarled and painful feet. Someone may be blind. Find your own level—it might be right down on the ground, or sitting or standing—and pull yourself painfully along. How does it feel to be a leper? Other people don't want contact with you. You are despised, unclean. How do you feel about your own body? Which parts of you are affected? Are you ashamed? Or resigned? Are you hopeful or have you lost hope by now? Do you want to look out at others or are you more used to looking at the ground? Does it hurt to walk along? How does the glare of the hot sun affect you?"

As they find their way into the role, note the variety of positions and movements they are using. Without being over-directive or too critical at this early stage, give plenty of encouragement to experiment with a variety of movements, helping by your own flow of words to encourage as much stimulus to the imagination as possible. Remember to break every few minutes as the group will probably be using much effort and tension in these particular movements. Encourage the use of space, different levels, different kinds of movement, different speeds. Encourage them to involve their thinking, feeling and facial expression too.

After some individual experimenting in movement like this, let them group together. "Do you think you'd want to relate to others in your group who are also lepers? You have to live together but is it a sharing, caring, relating group? How might you try to relate to another leper? Try it now. What are you saying to him with your actions? Now show how you might move forward as a group: edging, shuffling, moaning perhaps, pulling yourself along, hobbling. What are you thinking about? Now someone comes towards you—show how you would shrink away in alarm and fear. Habit dies hard and you have learnt to avoid healthy people. Your disease might spread to others unless you steer clear of them and you are feared, unwanted, unclean."

After a short break, suggest how the narrative in movement

might begin. Using a slow, flat beat on a drum, ask the lepers to enter from one side as a dishevelled, straggling group, until they reach the centre, where they pause. They might come in at different levels, some hobbling, some pulling themselves along in a sitting position, some crawling. Now use three single consecutive movements to depict the lepers' plight:

(i) Four slow drum beats—lepers slowly and disconsolately look at their own bodies, arms, legs.

Rattle of bells—lepers quickly recoil, hiding their faces in distaste.

(ii) Four drum beats—lepers try to relate to each other with a gesture (looking, sharing, inviting, imploring, etc.)

Rattle of bells—they turn quickly away back to their individual loneliness.

(iii) Four drum beats—some lepers stretch out their arms to the sky, others in front of them as though asking for help.

Rattle of bells—they quickly draw back in despair.

4. MORE DISCUSSION: JESUS ENTERS THE VILLAGE

Now break for more discussion about Jesus's entry into the village. We don't know if his disciples were with him on that occasion. It would seem quite permissible to use a few of the group as disciples, depending partly on the number of people taking part, and then it would be necessary to discuss what part they are going to play, their relationship to Jesus and the lepers, etc. In this example I am not going to discuss their part.

So now discuss the lepers' encounter with Jesus. How would they view this man? Would he seem to them 'ordinary' or unusual? How might they react to him? What variety of emotions might they express—fear? curiosity? hope? suspicion? Would they want to use speech at this point or remain silent? One effective device to use is that of 'voice percussion' where speech is used rhythmically, here to give a cumulative effect to produce tension and point out the contrast between the lepers and Jesus. A drum accompaniment may or need not be used. The lepers say these lines together, starting slowly and quietly and increasing in speed and volume (though avoid a hysterical shrieking). Each phrase is spoken four times:

"What is it? What is it? What is it? What is it?"
"Who's coming?" (four times)
"Jesus." (four times)
"Don't touch us!" (four times)
"Lepers!" (four times)
"Pity!" (four times)

As they speak so, as a group, they huddle together and shrink away from the presence of Jesus, fearful yet wondering at his calm, untroubled and authoritative presence. It is usually easier to learn the voice percussion separately, then fit it to the shrinking movements afterwards.

If the person who is to take the part of Jesus has already been chosen, he can practise walking in from the side opposite to the lepers then standing in a fairly central position facing them, so that they can, as a group, sensitise and react to him. Otherwise the producer can stand in *pro tem*. Sometimes further discussion is helpful at this stage. "What do you think you personally might find arresting and different about this man as he looked at you?" Different individuals may have distinct thoughts about the person of Jesus and the impression he would make upon them and the different ways they might react to him. Encourage group members to contribute freely in discussion and, as far as possible, use their ideas. In this way they will become increasingly involved and united as a group and will gradually lose any self-consciousness they had at the beginning.

Now try the movement through from the start. If anyone seems particularly restricted in movement, make a few suggestions to help him extend his range of movements.

5. THE LEPERS ARE HEALED

Allow time for a fairly leisurely discussion of this part of the narrative, pondering over the group's questions and comments and trying together to visualise something of what might have happened. Luke does not give any detail of this particular healing. Was there individual encounter or conversation? Did Jesus touch them "as they went" as often he did in healing individuals? How did they respond to his command to go and show themselves to the priests? How did they react to their healing? Would they react in different ways? What was the place of faith in this act of healing and how was it expressed? There will be much discussion here. Since the narrative lacks detail, it seems permissible to allow for some interpretation, provided the integrity of the narrative as given is in no way destroyed.

It might be that some, at this point, are tempted to try too hard with the action so that they strike a pose that looks artificial and over-dramatic, since few, if any, of the group will ever have had personal experience of physical healing. I sometimes ask them to think of some of their inner attitudes or needs which they would want to expose to Christ's healing touch (e.g. fear, jealousy, inferiority, a broken relationship). "If Jesus came into this room now, what would *I* ask of him in the area of healing?" Then—without naming aloud what they are thinking of—they might consider how they themselves would react to him. One person, the 'touch-hungry', might want to rush to him and clutch him whilst another might hang back nervously, fearful of close contact. One might long to have eye-to-eye contact with Jesus whilst another might avoid looking. One might walk straight towards him whilst another made a devious journey around the room, summoning the courage to approach him. Because we are constituted with such different temperaments we would make different approaches. I have found that by personalising the narrative at this important point, the feeling that "we must pretend to be lepers asking for healing" is superseded by a personal identification showing great integrity and validity.

Jesus could remain standing in a central position whilst the lepers, huddled to one side, might individually or in pairs slowly make their way past him at different levels, each receiving some recognition or affirmation, a touch or a healing look, assistance to stand up, or a word. As they move past him to the other side of the room so they discover they are healed. They look at their limbs, so recently wasted with disease and now healthy, they show their healed bodies to each other, they begin to rejoice and relate in a new way. The details of this sequence will need to be worked out in different ways by different groups. Whoever takes the part of Jesus will need to be very sensitive to the different needs of each leper as he asks for healing. This part of the narrative should not be rushed, though if it is too slow and drawn out the tension can become almost too great and prolonged. Music can helpfully be used for the healing—preferably a slow, even piece with a rich melody, such as part of Elgar's "Nimrod" from the *Enigma Variations*.

6. DANCE OF JOY

The lepers, now healed, are on the opposite side of the room from where they were originally, with Jesus looking at them. A simple dance of joy and restoration could be worked out here, perhaps a circle dance using generous arm movements, sweeping up, out and round to depict joy and wholeness. After this, the healed lepers could run out in twos and threes. Perhaps the last one might pause, look at Jesus, then run out with the rest but return in order to thank Jesus. Ask the group who would particularly like to return to give thanks—perhaps someone could do it with real personal conviction. Would he run straight up to Jesus or break his run and kneel to look at him or kneel to kiss his feet? Would Jesus touch him, speak to him or respond in some way? Such details could be worked out between the thankful Samaritan and Jesus.

Now put the whole movement together, including percussion effects, voice percussion and music, and preface by a reading of the narrative. As described here, it will probably not take more than six minutes or so. There will then need to be more group discussion, planning, adapting, practice of movements, grouping, etc. Different people can continue to offer comments and suggestions but, obviously, the producer should be prepared to make final decisions and give ultimate direction.

7. USES

What are some of the possible uses to which a piece of movement like this might be put?

(i) It could be used as part of a sermon in a church service, either preceded or followed by a verbal exposition. Just as a preacher or teacher sometimes uses visual aids to reinforce or clarify what he is saying, so this would be a means of reinforcement whereby you are addressing the eyes as well as the ears of a congregation. Obviously, in this case, the preacher needs to have seen the drama beforehand and discussed it with the group so that there is a unity between them.

We included this particular piece of drama in the Series III Service of Holy Communion and the main focus of the service was on Jesus the Healer. The hymns and Bible readings all pointed to various aspects of Christ's healing ministry and the administration of the sacraments came to us, on that occasion, as a most healing means of grace after a poignant visual reminder of those aspects of our humanity which stand in need of Christ's healing work.

(ii) The dramatised story might also be used as part of a longer, composite piece to depict one aspect of Christ's ministry on earth. We worked out an anthology on the life of Christ, called "With Love from Jesus", lasting one hour. We wanted in one section to portray something of his ministry to people through teaching and healing and chose three representative gospel narratives: the healing of the lepers, the forgiving of the adulterous woman and the welcome of the prodigal son. (The full outline of this can be found in chapter 8.) This particular anthology was used in several churches as a special guest service.

(iii) Another way of using this material might be to work out a more contemporary interpretation whilst still using the original narrative as the basic foundation. Thanks to modern medicine, there have been great advances in leprosy control. But there are other sicknesses which spoil individuals and society today. Loneliness, hatred and fear are only three of the twentieth-century illnesses which, like leprosy, continue to spoil and cripple our humanity, both individually and corporately. These, or other ills, might be portrayed through music, movement and readings (some written by group members) with consequent healing. If integrity is going to be observed, it is important here to look very carefully at the interpretation to see that each part of it rings true and does not contradict the teaching of Christ.

(iv) Obviously, this kind of dramatic work does not necessarily require an audience to make it effective. It could be used by a group who were studying Jesus's healing ministry, or for a weekend workshop with times for Bible study, prayer, discussion and ministry or to preface a time of prayer and intercession. It could be prepared for a youth club's 'think spot' or as an outcome of an R.E. lesson in school or for an assembly. I have sometimes used it with groups as a way in to the use of biblical narratives for drama and dance and have been surprised at how it has helped people to discuss their own needs for healing in such a way that we could pray and minister without pretence or cover-up.

On one occasion, when a group of Christian social workers had met together for a weekend conference and 'braved' some dramatic work, an older lady who walked painfully with sticks, due to arthritic hip joints, had come to the conference feeling very low and depressed. However, she decided to 'join in' the drama since she could do quite a lot without running or jumping, and she took the part of one of the lepers. Before our final run-through she quietly whispered to me that, when she made her way to Jesus for healing, she was going to leave her sticks at his feet and walk towards the healed lepers unaided. I was both interested and wondering about what would happen and decided not to interfere —I was not sure if she was expecting a physical healing but was aware of her very determined approach to the work in hand. But she did exactly as she intended, left her sticks, received a wonderfully compassionate touch from the chaplain who was taking the part of Jesus, and with a quiet radiance walked unaided to the other rejoicing lepers. She did not receive a physical healing but, as we prayed and sang together, her depression was completely lifted and during the rest of the weekend she reflected a peace and joy which greatly strengthened her attitude towards her own body and was a source of inspiration to others. The lady who took the part of the thankful Samaritan leper resorted to a corner of the room just before we were going to begin and bowed her head—I wondered why. Afterwards she told us that, before she acted the part, she needed to confess in prayer to a resentful spirit which she did not want to spoil the group's portrayal. After the weekend another wrote of depression having been lifted, faith strengthened and a new capacity to share the experience with others.

On another occasion, working with the same story in a student workshop in a theological college, we paused at the end for reflection and prayer. Many students spontaneously gave thanks to God for the power of Christ as they had experienced it that day, healing attitudes, blockages, fears and anxieties. They also spoke very movingly of new insights they had gained into a well-known narrative as well as the spirit of sharing, caring and creativity which had grown in the group over a day and a half of working together. Such examples help to point out the real involvement and therapeutic aspects of such group work. Whereas understanding a passage or incident involves important cerebral and mental processes this is not the sum total of learning. It is easy to deny our emotions and bodies, to suppress them as though they had little to do with understanding. But the fullest learning will have points of application for every part of our human nature, body, mind and spirit. It is possible to read of Jesus's healing ministry and treat it as a mental exercise only, without asking "How does this narrative or teaching affect me today with my needs?" When the whole person, body, mind and spirit, becomes involved in a piece of learning, as can often happen with this kind of dramatisation, the truths of the message find many points of entrance and opportunities for learning in depth become maximised.

Once, when working with a group of women in a religious community, it was suggested that, instead of them coming to Jesus as lepers in need of healing, they might like to bring with them (in imagination) someone who was sick or needy, and that this could be used as an intercession. One of them walked slowly along with one arm held up as though supporting someone else around the shoulders. Afterwards she seemed very moved and told me how she came from a family whose members were undemonstrative in showing affection to each other. This was the first time she had been able to "put an arm around her father" in intention and desire and gently bring him with her into the healing presence of Christ. For her, it was an experience of release.

Indeed, God's Word is powerful, like a sword which reaches down deep inside a person, disturbing, hurting, challenging but also healing, renewing and illumining. This kind of group work can certainly allow for the Word to minister unexpectedly in areas of ourselves which we would sometimes deny or be unaware of. It probably goes without saying that if work is done in this area the leader/producer needs great sensitivity and an openness to the Holy Spirit to know how to proceed.

CHAPTER 5

Scenes and Themes

HAVING EXAMINED ONE narrative in detail and seen how it can be dramatised, we go on in this chapter to look at a wider variety of ideas which a producer and group could explore together and adapt to their own uses. Generally they are short in length, planned to last only a few minutes each. Some could be incorporated into church services (e.g. a dramatised Bible reading), or used to introduce a thematic study or 'think spot'. Songs or poems might be used, solo or group, with supporting mime or dance, or psalms spoken by an individual or chorus with movement included. Also suggested—though not for public presentation—are some 'visual meditations' which the dance drama group might use for their own input, discussion and prayer. These might also be used in other kinds of fellowship groups or house groups.

1. BIBLE NARRATIVES

Both Old and New Testaments are full of narrative accounts which are dramatic, colourful and full of action and human interest. Some, such as Moses and the Israelites crossing the Red Sea, might entail considerable headaches for any producer and probably more high drama than was imagined! Others, however, such as the healing of the ten lepers, can be presented in a simple yet effective way so that God's truth is seen, heard and remembered. Parts of the story of Jonah could be dramatised without having to hire a whale, so that the message of Jonah's reluctance and God's faithfulness still comes across. The fall of man, as

78

narrated in Genesis chapter 3, could be effectively interpreted through reading, music, mime and dance and possibly followed by a short talk drawing out the implications of the fall and man's sin. In the following chapters different Bible stories and themes are described and worked out. At this stage we look at a few starters, some of which will be fully scripted and others simply suggested for a producer or group to work out in detail.

(a) Simon the Pharisee and Mary (Luke 7:36–50)

The theme of this narrative is Forgiveness.

Cast: Simon   Mary
      Three guests   Singer
      Jesus   Narrator

(It is visually helpful if part of the action can take place on two levels above the ground, either steps, acting blocks or two tiers of small platforms.)

NARRATOR: "One of the Pharisees asked Jesus to eat with him, and he went into the Pharisee's house, and sat at table. And a woman of the city, who was a sinner, when she learned that he was sitting at table in the Pharisee's house, brought an alabaster flask of ointment."

Jesus enters DSL with Simon slightly ahead of him, pointing the way to his house, and three of his guests. (Down stage left= performers' left-hand side.)

SIMON: "Teacher, come and eat with us."

Together they mount the steps and sit down, reclining as at a meal. As they are settling, Mary enters either from a side aisle or entrance DSR. She comes in tentatively, aware that she has not been invited, yet also concerned to find Jesus. She is carefully cupping her hands (wrists together, fingers cupped up), as though carrying a precious flask of ointment. As she approaches, Simon stands and points to her, annoyed by her intrusion, and his guests turn to whisper with each other. Jesus leans forward as though to welcome her warmly. As she looks towards him, wanting to come nearer, Simon and his guests turn away in distaste with hard expressions and stiffened shoulders, necks and arms. Either on tape or live, they repeat their opinion of Mary in turn:

SIMON: "Street woman!"

GUEST 1: "Sinner!"

GUEST 2: "Unclean!"

GUEST 3: "Prostitute!"

(Repeat sequence three times in all, briskly and clearly.)

(This sequence sounds effective if previously taped since it is meant to indicate their thoughts rather than their actual speech. Their bodily positions should show the censorious nature of their thinking.)

Mary recoils, aware of their thoughts yet still longing for contact with Jesus who remains looking at her without moving.

At this point, singer (or group) sings a song to show some of the thoughts in Mary's mind, whilst she performs a simple dance which Jesus and the others watch. If possible, one of the group should write a song depicting Mary's desire to come to Jesus, her love for him, also her awareness of her sins, her fear of those who judge and expose her, yet her great longing to give him something costly in order to express her gratitude. Mary should use the floor space in front of the others for her dance, making stretching movements towards Jesus, reaching upwards with her flask, expressing joy, love and contrition. Wherever she moves, she should keep looking back at Jesus and retaining eye contact with him and he with her. Eventually, as the song ends, she approaches the group, still watching Jesus and carefully cupping her hands. Simon and his guests move back, critical yet curious. Mary kneels down by Jesus's feet, raises her hands high, wrists together, then ripples her fingers down, as though the liquid is flowing on to Jesus's feet. She then gently wipes his feet with her long hair whilst Jesus quietly looks on, moved by her act of love. Simon and the others look disapproving.

JESUS: "Simon, I have something to say to you."

SIMON: "What is it, teacher?"

JESUS: "A certain creditor had two debtors; one owed five hundred denarii, and the other fifty. When they could not pay, he forgave them both. Now which of them will love him more?"

SIMON: "The one to whom he forgave more, I suppose."

JESUS: "You are right. Do you see this woman? I entered your house, you gave me no water for my feet, but she has wet my feet with her tears and wiped them with her hair. You gave me no kiss, but from the time I came in she has not ceased to kiss my feet. You did not anoint my head with oil, but she has anointed my feet with ointment. Therefore I tell you, her sins, which are many, are forgiven, for she loved much, but he who is forgiven little, loves little."

(Jesus then stands with Mary kneeling in front of him, looking into his face.)

JESUS: "Your sins are forgiven. Your faith has saved you; go in peace." (He lays his hands on her head. She gives him one more grateful look then exits DSR. Jesus watches her go, turns to look at Simon and his guests and exits DSL. As he leaves, one of the guests asks Simon, with an expression of criticism mixed with curiosity,)

GUEST: "Who is this, who even forgives sins?"
(The group exit DSL, shrugging their shoulders.)

(b) *Jesus heals a blind man* (*Mark 8: 22-30*)

Here is a simple outline which could possibly be worked out in detail by producer and group members. The use of children is optional but could be enjoyable for the occasional 'all-age' activity.

Cast: Group of village men   Jesus
        Group of village women   Group of disciples
        A few children   One drum player
        Blind man

(i) *Village scene:* To a suitable piece of background music (e.g. a piece of Jewish folk music), different groups of villagers meet in the street and pass the time of day. A few women might mime bringing their water pots to the well to draw water and talk together. Some men sit nearby repairing fishing nets whilst some children play hop-scotch or accompany their parents. A blind man sits alone by the roadside with his begging-bowl.

Suddenly someone runs in with the news, "Jesus is coming!" (This could be taken up by others who excitedly pass the news round until, with a rhythmic drum beat, it becomes a chorus spoken in unison by the villagers.)

(ii) *Jesus and his disciples arrive:* As they enter Bethsaida, people crowd round in curiosity, all except the blind man who is left sitting on his own, wondering what is happening. One of the crowd then goes to fetch him and the rest make a way for him to be brought to Jesus. Perhaps to their surprise, even disappointment, Jesus leads him away from the crowd, the disciples following. He is not wanting to attract attention as a wonder-worker.

Jesus puts spittle on the man's eyes then lays his hands upon them. He asks, "Do you see anything?" Looking up, the man says he can, in a blurred way. "I see men; but they look like trees, walking." Jesus again lays hands on his eyes and this time he can see clearly. Jesus tells him to go home without re-entering the village.

(iii) *Jesus is the Messiah:* Jesus and his disciples continue their journey and on the way he asks them what people are saying about who he really is (see Mark 8:27–30). During this piece of dialogue, possibly a quiet backing of music could be used which, after the declaration that Jesus is the Christ, the awaited Messiah, could be used as a group song by the disciples (e.g. "Son of God", *Sound of Living Waters*, p. 43). Jesus could stand amongst them and they could sing and use a few worshipful movements indicating his Lordship.

This scheme could either be used as an improvisation exercise during a rehearsal session, or it could be worked out more thoroughly and scripted as a short dramatisation.

(c) *The fellowship of the first Christians (Acts 2:44–47)*

It makes an interesting exercise to study this short passage together and use it as a basis for mime and movement, possibly with music or single words used percussively, but otherwise not using dialogue. Some of the themes which appear and which could be worked out in pairs, small groups or the large group are: unity, sharing, generous giving, worship, eating together with joy and thanksgiving, praising God, welcoming others who come and join the fellowship. Some of these ideas overlap and plenty of discussion is needed to explore their content and meaning, then link them together to achieve a cumulative group effect. In what ways did the quality of their life together attract others to them and how could this be portrayed in movement? There is plenty of scope here for discussion, prayer, movement work and grouping and, like the last suggestion, it could be a useful longer improvisation exercise for a rehearsal. Otherwise, it might be used during a group retreat where the topic for the day is Fellowship.

Other Bible stories which are suitable for dramatisation are listed in Appendix B.

2. THEMES

As well as the many Bible narratives which can be presented visually, themes emerging from them can also be explored. In the story of Simon the Pharisee and Mary, the theme of Forgiveness comes through poignantly. A group working on this could find it helpful to discuss different aspects of the theme which might complement this particular story. What does it mean in experience to be forgiven and what responses does it evoke? What does it mean to forgive another person? What did Jesus mean when he taught that we should be ready to forgive not only seven times but "seventy times seven" (Matthew 18:22)? What does it mean to us, as Christians, that God has forgiven us for Christ's sake?

Or take two contrasting themes such as Bondage and Freedom. These are prominent throughout the whole Bible. In the Old Testament, both for individuals and for the whole nation of Israel, there is a dramatic progression from slavery to the promised freedom of Canaan. In the New Testament much of Jesus's teaching about the Kingdom of God involves a turning from different kinds of bondage and a growth into different kinds of freedom, spiritual, emotional and physical (e.g. Luke 8:26–39, Luke 4:16–21, Matthew 12:22–32). He taught that "If the Son makes you free, you will be free indeed". St. Paul also uses these themes, stating that the whole created world, including nature and humanity, is in a state of "bondage to decay" waiting with an eager longing to obtain their "glorious liberty" which is to come (Romans 8:18–25). Use a Bible Concordance to discover the many references to these themes, which would make an excellent basis for group study and interpretation. Consider together the different kinds of bondage evident in society today, at international and national levels, in the local community and amongst individuals. Discuss what freedom is, bearing in mind both 'freedom from' various conditions and 'freedom for'. Is freedom simply a lack of restraints or does it also include a certain discipline and responsibility? How can these themes be interpreted in movement? We often found that it seemed easier to portray bondages than freedoms (perhaps because we were more used to living with them?) and our freedom in Christ needed considerable discussion, prayer, exploration and disciplined group work. It might be fun to enjoy an abandoned caper or a few leaps in the air, but does this really communicate freedom? We discovered a need to experiment more with disciplined limbering exercises, movement vocabulary and body control. There is far more form and symmetry to freedom than might be imagined.

Many of these themes emerge in a contemporary way when we start thinking of current pressures, both group and individual. There are the bondages of war, oppression, rejection, hatred, conflict. In thinking about these words and trying to portray them through mime and movement, people will tend to strike certain postures (which might express the bondage well) but soon run out of ideas and movement vocabulary. In exploring an abstract concept it is best to think of as many concrete situations as possible in order to see its outworking and effects. For example, on the theme of conflict, here is the poignant opening of a news feature from Belfast:

(a) *"Out of the rubble of Belfast . . ."*

Belfast, Northern Ireland.
A shattered city, a divided country. Where the way of moderation is strangled at every turn.
Where ignorant Catholics kill bigoted Protestants in the cause of political 'freedom', where ignorant Protestants kill bigoted Catholics in the cause of 'religious' liberty.
Where Christians, Catholic and Protestant, weep for the cause of Jesus Christ.
And where people live, and young men and women still

manage to fall in love. (George Target, *Church of England News-paper*, May 1974.)

This could be worked out as a piece of dramatic movement and mime to illustrate the conflict theme. We did this in a workshop and followed it with a time of prayer for Ireland and individuals we knew there. Newspaper headlines are often dramatic and can spark the imagination. A group could be given the task of collecting headlines, articles or stories illustrating a particular theme, bring them to a rehearsal for sharing then select what might be suitable for dramatisation. In this way, an abstract concept can be made concrete and communicated more effectively.

(b) *Refugees*

Another aspect of the Bondage theme is famine. Here is a description of a piece of dramatic movement which portrays the needs of refugees in famine-struck areas. It is prefaced by a personal account of a visit to refugee camps in India, made by the Rev. George Hoffman, Director of TEAR Fund, one of the many Relief Agencies working for needy areas.

Cast: Ten refugees, including at least two men   Narrator
                                                        Singer (optional)
(The movement could be adapted to include more or fewer dancers.)

Music: Finale (Adagio Lamentoso) of Symphony no. 6 (*Pathétique*) by Tchaikovsky. The movement can be fitted to the music so that both end together. The producer is advised to work this out carefully beforehand and script the movement accordingly.

Introduction: The refugees take up still positions in a wide semi-circle shape, each depicting need, stress, poverty or despair. A few could be holding simple wooden bowls and one woman is clutching a small baby wrapped in a cloth. Vary the levels and positions. Whilst the Narrator reads, the refugees remain still.

NARRATOR: "As you go through the streets of Calcutta there are people cleaning their teeth in the gutter, washing themselves in the gutter and doing other things in the gutter. In fact the whole street at times seems to be one great toilet and bathroom combined.

As you get near to the camps on the edge of the city it seems at first indescribable—it is just a vast sea of mud and people ankle-deep. The first thing you notice, as quite opposed to the streets of India normally, nobody begs—there seems to be just a resigned look on everyone's face, a look of horror on some, a look of fear on others, but mostly just a look of hopelessness.

"Situated near Dumdum Airport was Camp Sahara and it was well named. There was a sense of desolation which seemed to hang over the whole human wilderness and the feeling was quite overpowering. All around there was an eerie silence, whole families lay huddled together, too weak to move, grasping one another and sheltering under coverings of straw and twigs. Children and old people lay exhausted on rain-sodden mattresses. The stronger ones were queuing up at a pump which gurgled away with every creak of the handle. Some of the people we met had been on the move for twenty days before they reached the camp. Many of them were just crouching exhausted, lying in the mud and the rain. Some were sleeping in drain pipes, others living in ditches—any kind of covering as long as they could keep out the rain and the cold.

"At one field hospital, as we stood by the tent flap of a ward, a man collapsed in front of us as he was being brought in by his relatives. They dragged him into the ward and immediately he was surrounded by the doctor and nurses who put him on a saline drip. He was in the advanced stages of cholera, like many others on those wooden pallets inside. In that ward five people had died the day before. In the same ward five were born. The doctor kept brushing the flies off his patients as he walked round tending them. As we stepped outside this ward a queue of people surged towards us and two young girls raced across holding their babies. The tears were streaming down their faces as they reached over the barbed wire. They were desperate for some kind of help, anything that we could do, and as they held their babies up to us, just like skeletons with skin stretched across them, all we could do was turn and point to the queue. And the queue stretched for nearly a mile round the camp. I'll never forget the look of anguish and despair as we turned our backs and forced ourselves to walk away feeling absolutely helpless.

"There was another occasion as a missionary took us round the camp where the refugees were registering. As we were getting back into the jeep, I can remember I couldn't move my legs. I looked down and there was a woman wrapped around my ankles. She was holding my feet, kissing my feet, she wouldn't let go and the tears were streaming down her face. I turned to the missionary and said 'What can I do now?' He just pointed down to his ankles and there was another woman wrapped around him too.

"Strange, I can remember when we left Calcutta early in the morning to visit these camps, our conversation was animated as we chatted to one another and told each other of our experiences. On the return journey, as we left the camps, a silence seemed to settle over the truck and we stared past one another, not wanting to look into each other's faces or notice each other's watery eyes."

As the reading ends, fade up music.

(i) The refugees slowly and painfully rise or turn to look at each other with expressions of misery and isolation.

(ii) One refugee, holding a food bowl, moves slowly round to each of the group in turn asking for food, but everyone is in the same plight and they turn away from her.

(iii) She moves to the centre of the group, facing the congregation, reaching out with her bowl first to those refugees on her left then to those on her right.

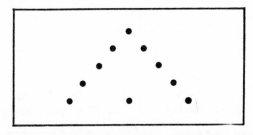

(iv) She staggers, faint with hunger and falls to her knees, then pulls herself up and turns in a slow swirl of misery.

(v) She moves DSL, her bowl extended in one hand, as though asking the congregation to help her. Her head is bowed on to her other arm. She repeats the same movement DSR then moves slowly across stage left to join in the semi-circle with the others.

(vi) In turn, starting from the left end, each refugee slowly turns to the one on his right, imploring food. (The last in the semi-circle hides his head in despair.)

(vii) Then, starting from the right end, each couple turns to each other, indicating need, hunger, despair, then they again turn away, hiding their faces.

(viii) Alternate refugees in the semi-circle reach up, as if to implore God's help, whilst others reach out in the direction of the congregation.

(ix) The solo refugee moves again to the centre, with one hand stretches out to the congregation and with the other indicates the needy group, as if beseeching on their behalf. As there is no response, she shakes her head in despair, reaches up to the heavens with her bowl, falls to her knees and repeats her action, then slowly she drags herself to the right of the group and falls huddled.

(x) Two other refugees move slowly forward, one beckoning the other. The first kneels down and supports the collapsed refugee against her, whilst the other offers her bowl to lick.

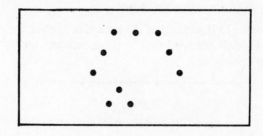

(xi) One of the refugees, a mother with her baby, now moves to the centre of the group, fumbling with her bundle and rocking. The baby's father stands by her side, an empty bowl in his hand.

(xii) Together they move round to different refugees in the group. The mother shows her starved child and the father indicates his empty bowl. Some shake their heads in sorrow, some turn away in resignation.

(xiii) The mother moves first to the left, facing the congregation, then to right, holding out her baby with a pleading gesture. (A few improvised movements might be included here, portraying her agony of spirit as she watches her baby starve to death. She holds out the child to the congregation, then up to God whilst the father looks on helplessly.)

(xiv) Suddenly, the mother looks at the baby closely and recoils. The father draws near to look, sees the child is dead, takes it from his wife and places the bundle on the ground. The mother kneels beside it, rocking with her face in her hands and weeping silently.

(xv) The other refugees move in a little to see what is happening and the mother moves amongst them, holding on to their legs, clutching at them, pointing to the dead child and imploring them.

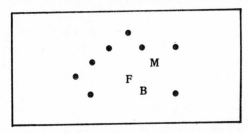

(xvi) One or two of the refugees pull themselves forward and touch the baby. The father leads his wife to the left side, seeking to comfort her. The child is left in the centre and the group becomes apathetic again in postures of despair and weakness.

(xvii) Slowly they rise to exit left, starting with the refugee DSR. Some shuffle out, others drag themselves off. One man falls and two others try to help him up but cannot move him. He is left lying beside the dead child whilst the rest make their exit. He remains there as the music fades, there is a slight pause then either a suitable solo could be sung or a poem read. We used a solo song, with simple guitar accompaniment, slow and sad like a cry from the heart, called "Lord, have mercy" (see Appendix A (i)). It was written and sung by one of the group and was a simple reflection of the dramatic portrayal, giving the congregation time to let the stark message be registered.

The slow twisted body-shapes used in this piece need considerable control and practice. It is also important to practise letting each part of the body, including facial expression, portray something of the misery and pain of body and spirit felt by the refugees. Of course, it is virtually impossible to show how grim it really is. Before performing this piece we would pray that God would keep us from phoney play-acting and help us so to identify with those who suffered like this that his Spirit of truth would communicate through us. Sometimes the actual pains of bodily tension in maintaining certain positions were a reminder to us of the far greater pains we were portraying.

Some other ideas for thematic dramatisation are listed in Appendix B.

3. SONGS AND POEMS

A song may be used to reinforce a theme portrayed by the group —as with the Refugees drama above. It can also be used in a recurring way during the dramatic movement to emphasise some aspect of the narrative. We took Sydney Carter's well-known song "When I needed a neighbour" as a recurring theme during a presentation of the Good Samaritan. A small group, standing to one side of the altar, sang part of it to a guitar accompaniment before the portrayal began. During the action the guitarist picked up the melody several times then, when the Samaritan came to minister to the man attacked by robbers, the organist resumed the melody and improvised on it very effectively. The change in sound, whilst retaining the same melody, added to the dramatic portrayal in a moving way. At the end all the characters and the singing group made an exit down through the church's central aisle singing the refrain quite slowly and leaving the congregation with the challenge of the question, "When I needed a neighbour were you there?"

A similar thing might be attempted with the song "When he comes back" by Malcolm Stewart (*Faith, Folk and Festivity*, p. 2). The song is based on the parable of the wise and foolish virgins (Matthew 25:1–13) and could be used as a theme song that comes into the dramatised parable. Or it could be interpreted in simple movement and mime as it stands. Another song in the same collection, "The day of the Spirit", written for Pentecost, might be used in a similar way. Here the Spirit is celebrated as coming in wind and fire, filling with courage, disposing of fear and exploding in power. This suggests whirling movement and dance in glad response to the Holy Spirit's infilling. The song "Let the cosmos ring", also in this collection, is another song of celebration which could include dramatic portrayal. It is like a modern psalm, exhorting people in contemporary situations to offer praise. Mime and dance could be used to help convey the gladness of the music.

Group members who enjoy singing and playing different instruments should be encouraged to make their own collections of music, some composed by other musicians but some written by themselves. Two of our group knew they had good singing voices but were less aware that they could also write songs. With encouragement, prayer and a sifting of ideas they were able, either separately or together, to write songs which fitted well into various presentations by the group.

It can also bring some good surprises to encourage group members to experiment in writing verse on different themes. Although to start with people may offer verse which is very subjective and perhaps unoriginal, once a beginning has been made and a piece of writing attempted, with encouragement they can then go on to think more about form, style and vocabulary. At one drama workshop with a group of young wives, I suggested that the dramatic movement might be interspersed with suitable readings. My first suggestion that they might like to try writing verse or songs about different themes in the drama was met with some dismay and apprehension! It reminded some of failures at school. We discussed this and prayed that God's creative Spirit would keep us open to fresh possibilities. At the next rehearsal several poems and three songs were offered with some diffidence and we were, with a few changes, able to use them all. For some it came as a great encouragement that they could express themselves in this way.

It is also worth dipping into books of verse, both to see how poets use words in writing about certain themes and also to choose poems which might be on the same theme as a piece of dramatisation, to use as a meditation or reflection during a presentation. I am not suggesting that verse which has been written for its own sake is misused by being 'dragged into' a piece of drama or dance. At the same time, the reading of a poem which both picks up the same theme as a piece of drama or dance and is also heard for its own sake, seems both permissible and helpful. For some observers the theme will make its impression visually, for others verbally. Have a look at some of the verse in *That Way and This—Poetry for Creative Dance* and other anthologies of religious verse, both of which might give further ideas for the use of verse in conjunction with drama and dance.

4. PSALMS

The Old Testament Psalms present us with a wonderfully rich variety of Jewish poetry ranging over a wide spectrum of human experience and emotions. There are some full of praise and worship and others whose chief theme is contrition and penitence. In some the writer rejoices in victory and triumph and in others he voices his depression and sense of God's absence. Above all they are personal expressions which still have much to say to people today. The *Living Bible* paraphrases the Psalms in a striking way impressing well-known phrases with vigour and relevance and either this or the Revised Standard Version is recommended for use by the Narrator.

Many of the Psalms could be read either by one person or by a group in choral verse speaking and accompanied by dramatic movement or mime. Psalm 107, for example, has as its theme God our Deliverer. It consists largely of four dramatic cameos showing different kinds of human need and God's deliverance from those needs. Derek Kidner, in his commentary on the Psalms, writes, "The centre-piece of this striking psalm is the set of four word-pictures of human predicaments and divine interventions."[1] After an introduction (1–3) which sets the psalm in its context of Israel's deliverance from exile, the writer describes the four groups and Kidner sub-titles these as follows:

vv. 4–9   Wanderers retrieved
10–16   Prisoners released
17–22   The sick restored
23–32   The storm-tossed rescued.

In each of these pictures there is a clear pattern which should be used to guide the dramatic movement or mime. (i) People are in need. (ii) They cry out to God. (iii) He delivers them. (iv) They express their thanksgiving. In the final section of the psalm (33–43) God is seen to be the Lord of the whole earth.

Here is the outline of a dramatised reading of Psalm 107.

Cast: Narrator   Group C (Sick)—five
Group A (Wanderers)—six   Group D (Storm-tossed)—four
Group B (Prisoners)—five   Storm group—eight–ten
(The size of these groups can be varied.)

Narrator	Dramatic movement
Narrator stands in the pulpit or to one side of the groups.	The four groups (A–D) take up their positions in front of the congregation. Each holds a still group position until their turn comes to move. Use different levels in each group—standing, sitting, kneeling, lying down.

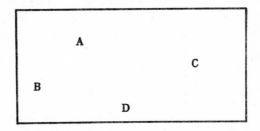

Group A kneel or stand, backs to the congregation. They look weary and despondent.

Group B sit, kneel or stand with wrists together as though bound and captive. One stands with fists clenched to God.

Group C hold positions of sickness and pain. One supports another.

Group D sit in a line, one behind another, as if in a boat. The storm group are off stage left.

Reads vv. 1–3 4, 5	Groups remain still, holding their positions. Group A wander, as though lost. They are hungry, faint and dispirited.
6a	After v. 6a has been read, Group A fall, some to the ground, some to their knees, reaching out to God with cries such as "Lord, help us—", "Lead us—", "Show us the way—", etc.
6b, 7	God has heard their cry. One of the group rises and beckons the others to their feet, pointing with hope to the way ahead. They help each other forward, moving around the other groups with eager expressions until they return to their former place where they kneel in gratitude and praise.
8	Group A recite v. 9 together with hands stretched

Narrator	Dramatic movement
	out in thanksgiving to God. They then hold a still position again, but this time with heads up.
10, 11	Group B show their bound wrists and fumble around in the dark. Some attempt to shake their fists at God.
12	They stoop down in oppression, hiding their faces.
13a	After v. 13a has been read, Group B cry out to God, "Lord, forgive us—", "Have mercy—", "Lord, deliver us—", etc.
13b, 14	One by one they are freed from their bonds, stretching out their hands and arms and stretching. They
15	look at each other with joy.
	Group B recite v. 16 together, raising their arms. They then return to a still position.
17, 18	Group C show their twisted and deformed bodies. Some reach out towards the other groups as though appealing for help.
19a	After v. 19a has been read, Group C all look up seeking God's help. "Lord, heal us—", "Make us well", "Lord, cleanse us—", etc.
19b, 20	Two of the group, linked together, reach up their hands, receive God's healing and gradually stretch
21	upright in delight. The rest find healing also.
	Group C recite v. 22 together then move joyfully across to join with Groups A and B.
23, 24	Group D make rowing movements together.
25–28a	The 'storm group' swirl in DSL, surrounding Group D with wind and wave movements. (Waves can be shown by three people kneeling on their heels and swaying backwards and forwards with arms swooping up and forwards over their heads. Behind these three are three more, standing and making similar movements with the arms and bending at the knees, in a ski-ing movement, feet slightly apart. The wind can be two people swirling and dancing around the waves.)
	After v. 28a has been read, Group D cry out, "Lord save us—", "Protect us!", "Lord, we're drowning!",
28b, 29	etc. The wind and waves subside.

Narrator	Dramatic movement
30, 31	Group D resume their rowing.
	Group D recite v. 32 together and move across to join the others.
33, 34	The four groups now stand in one circle, facing outwards. Together they bend forward, faces in hands then together bring their hands quickly down to each side of their bodies in a slashing or 'cancelling' movement.
35	Still in the same circle, they cup their hands at chest-level (35a) and quickly lift them up and 'flicker' their fingers down, like water (35b).
36	They turn to face inwards, kneeling on their heels.
37, 38	With their hands, they make scattering movements into the circle.
39, 40	Suddenly they cower back, huddling closer and one or two point out of the circle, as though indicating the 'princes'.
41	They stand, facing outwards, in a circle.
42	They raise their arms, holding hands around the circle.
	They quickly move out of the circle, all face the congregation in a semi-circular group, extend right arms and recite together v. 43.

There are many exciting possibilities in presenting different psalms which will help fix them in people's minds and encourage them to re-read them. Christian Arts Project have scripted Psalms 73 and 148 effectively and the reader is recommended to consider these also. (See Appendix B.)

5. VISUAL MEDITATIONS

Finally in this chapter, we look at a few examples of 'visual meditations'. These are not presentations in the sense of having a congregation or audience present, but rather pieces of Bible-centred group work. The aim is for a group to read the Bible passages and meditate on them in such a way that the truth of

God enters and affects each part of them—mind, emotions, body and will. They are not gimmicks but a way of learning by doing and giving God's Spirit access to the whole person. Obviously, they are not suitable for every fellowship group and leaders should exercise discrimination about using them and should also check out people's reactions afterwards.

(a) *The Lord is My Shepherd (Psalm 23)*

This activity is for any even number of people.

Timing: About one hour.

Things needed: Bible for each person.

Blindfold scarves for half the group.

Objects pleasant to feel (e.g. smooth pebbles, piece of wood bark, feather, orange, etc.).

Simple items of food and drink (e.g. chocolate, sandwich, apple, water, etc.).

Sounds pleasant to hear (e.g. birdsong, recorder, water from tap, music on tape or record, etc.).

Pleasant smells (e.g. rose or other flowers, etc.).

Setting: Almost any premises might be used, though ideally somewhere where there is space to wander outside and inside (e.g. church premises or a fairly large house and garden).

Introduction (15 minutes): This well-known psalm, rich in shepherd imagery, describes how God leads and cares for his people. It is helpful to understand something about a Palestinian shepherd and his role (see a Bible dictionary or commentary on the Psalms) and to study this psalm together so that its facts are clear first. When this has been done go on to discover what such a quality of shepherding might feel like. It is one thing to understand this mentally and another to know the trustful experience of being led.

Activity (20 minutes): This 'trust walk' gives an experience of being led and cared for. The group should divide into pairs. One person in each pair is blindfolded and the other acts as his guide. Conversation between them is minimal and limited to the guide giving a few instructions when necessary, or reassurances. The guide can take his partner anywhere, leading him by the arm and protecting him from mishap or collision. The role of the guide is

"Whoever comes to me shall never be hungry" (John 6:35)

"The fountain in my garden . . . pouring down from Lebanon"
(Song of Songs 4:15)

Jesus and the adulterous woman

Conflict

Crucifixion

The prodigal son in
the far country

The prodigal,
his thoughts
and his father

The prodigal returns
home

The father's welcome

The thankful leper

"On your belly you shall crawl, and dust you shall eat"
(Genesis 3:14)

"Surely he has borne our griefs and carried our sorrows"
(Isaiah 53:4)

"Let them praise his name with dancing" (Psalm 149:3)

to be a responsible and caring 'shepherd' so that his partner can have complete trust in him. The guide may take him up steps or stairs, finding the best ways to lead him. He may give him something interesting to feel, such as a twig, or something to eat or drink. He may lead him around the garden and give him a flower to smell or ask him to stop and listen to some of the sounds of nature. He may leave him on his own for a few minutes but in a safe place or a chair and with the blindfolded person knowing for sure that his guide will return. Colliding, tripping, etc., should be avoided so that the person's assurance grows as he continues.

Still in the same couples, but with the blindfold now removed, each person now has ten minutes to describe to his partner how the experience felt. What was it like to be led around, completely dependent on someone else? What did it show that person about his ability to exercise trust? What did it feel like to do the guiding and be responsible for the other person? Did it throw any fresh light on Psalm 23 for either person?

Whole group: As a closing activity, pray together (5–10 minutes) using the psalm as a basis. Sing together "The Lord is my Shepherd".

(b) *The Fruit of the Spirit (Galatians 5: 13–25)*

Timing: 45 minutes.
Things needed: Bible for each person.
A bowl with enough pieces of fruit for each person to receive one (if this is rather expensive, small fruit such as cherries or grapes are suitable).
Sticky labels to write on.

Introduction (15 minutes): In this passage Paul explains what Christian freedom is about. Our freedom is not for self-satisfaction but that we might love others. In following this through Paul then goes on to contrast "walking in the flesh" to "walking in the Spirit". He lists those sinful attitudes and acts which run counter to the Kingdom of God, then lists those good characteristics which are the fruit of the Holy Spirit indwelling the Christian (vv. 22, 23). Using a commentary, first look at the different fruits, seeking to appreciate the meaning of each.

Activity (25 minutes): The group sits in a circle in silence. Someone passes round a bowl with enough fruit for each person to have one piece. On each fruit is stuck a small label with the name of one of the fruits of the Spirit written on it. (The writing should face the fruit so that it cannot be seen until removed. With small fruit, such as grapes, the labels are placed in a pile, name down, beside the fruit.) Each person takes a fruit, removes the label and spends five minutes meditating on that particular spiritual fruit and its application in his own life. After five minutes each turns to the person on his right, shares what he has received and his thoughts about it. Each person has ten minutes for this. Each then prays for the other and any particular situations in his life where this fruit is felt to be needed.

Whole group (5 minutes): Sing together "For the fruit of the Spirit is love, joy, peace" (the words follow the same order as vv. 22, 23. Instead of "against" in v. 23 (R.S.V.), "for" is sung.).

(c) *The Potter* (*Jeremiah 18:1–6*)

Timing: One hour–1¼ hours.
Things needed: Bible for each person.
Pile of newspapers.
Clay, plasticene or Playdo for each person.

Introduction (10 minutes): In this enacted parable, Jeremiah is instructed by God to watch a potter at work. As he moulds one of his pots it is spoiled so he remoulds it. This is what God does with his people. Whoever introduces this study should look at a Bible commentary on this passage.

Activity (45 minutes): Each person is given a newspaper (to keep the floor clean) and a lump of clay. He spends ten minutes moulding a pot into a shape and design which he feels to be less pleasing and attractive. At the end of the ten minutes he crushes the shape and spends ten to fifteen minutes remoulding it into a shape and design which he likes and finds pleasing. (If anyone finds this difficult or frustrating, he could roughly sketch the sort of design he intended in order to explain it.) Now each person turns to his neighbour, each sharing for ten minutes what he has made, what it felt like and anything which God seems to be saying through this illustration. (e.g. Have there been any 'moulding' experiences

lately which have felt either good or bad? Can you see how these
might become usable by God for you? Does it seem that any
particular changes are needful or desirable in you at present?) Pray
with and for each other using these verses and activity as a basis.

Whole group (5 minutes): Sing together "Spirit of the Living
God, fall afresh on me". An alternative to this activity which
stresses group relationships rather than the individual is as
follows:

Divide into smaller groups of four to five each, with a co-
ordinator in each. Each group spends ten to fifteen minutes experimenting with a group shape, interlocking bodies in order to portray
a jar of the group's chosen design. Several attempts can be made,
then, at the end of the fifteen minutes, each group shows its jar
shape to the others. Still in the smaller groups, for twenty minutes,
discuss with each other how the activity felt, then go on to share
some of the difficulties experienced in working/living/getting on
with each other in our occupations/families/churches. What do we
find hard in establishing good relationships and maintaining them?
How can we help each other to grow? (N.B. This is not an opportunity for gossip or criticism of others but a chance to face up to our
own difficulties and share them with others in a context of prayer
and care.) Spend about ten minutes in prayer for each other.

(d) *Foot-washing* (*John 13: 1–17*)

Timing: About one hour.
Things needed: Plastic bowl with water.
　　　　　　　　Sponge or cloth.
　　　　　　　　Towels.

Introduction (15 minutes): This event precedes the Last Supper
which Jesus took with his disciples before his arrest and trial. He
gives them an example of what it means to serve one another and
put the needs of others before one's own. Ordinarily when a host
invited guests to a meal water was provided at the entrance of his
house and servants would wash the guests' feet to refresh them
before eating. On this occasion Jesus deliberately identifies with
a servant, though he was their host and leader, to give to his
disciples a demonstration of Christian service. Refer to a Bible
commentary on these verses.

Activity (40 minutes): The group sits in a circle. Without talking, each takes the bowl of water, washes the feet of his neighbour and dries them. He resumes his seat and, after pausing to reflect on what has happened, the person who has had his feet washed does the same for his neighbour. (N.B. It is helpful to tell people before they begin what will happen, so that shoes, socks and tights can be removed beforehand.)

Afterwards, pause for five minutes so that each person can silently pray that God will show him someone to serve, through some act, conversation, letter, etc., in a way which will bring refreshment and caring.

Now let each turn to the next person and share, for ten minutes each, their reactions to the activity and anything they learnt through it. How did it feel to stoop down and serve? How did it feel to be served? Did it throw any fresh light on the narrative? Now pray for each other.

Whole group (5 minutes): Sing "The Foot Washing Song" (*Sound of Living Waters*, p. 230).

CHAPTER 6

Ideas for a Day or Weekend Workshop

THERE SEEMS TO be a particular value in a group of people getting away together in order to concentrate on some group activity, whether this be just for a day or for a longer period. Often the sheer change of place brings refreshment and when a group is working together at a project it can be very helpful to have longer than an hour or two for ideas to flow, creativity to spark and discussion and prayer to be included at a more leisurely rate than the usual weekly get-together. If a group is wanting to work out a contribution of dance for a particular church service, a day's concentrated work can often be more rewarding than several week-night sessions. Especially if a group is wanting to get to know each other better and really be in fellowship together, it is worth some careful forward planning to find a Saturday which everyone can set aside for this. Also the venue is important. If the place where you normally meet is adequate for space, reasonable warmth and comfort and with facilities for brewing coffee, this might be the best place. Otherwise there might be somewhere not too distant which you could use—another church's hall or a retreat centre might be possibilities.

In meeting together like this, the immediate aim might well be to work out a contribution for a service, but, if the group is going to work together in a satisfying, creative way, the dance or drama should not be seen as an isolated activity. It is helpful to include time for sharing, getting to know each other better, prayer and group study of Bible passages you may be interpreting in movement. Often I have discovered that it is as we share together in greater depth and grow to know and love each other that God's

Spirit works amongst and through us in creativity and freedom. Moreover, real group commitment, whatever form its display takes, is a powerful visual aid of loving fellowship, mutual trust and acceptance.

In this chapter we shall look at two possible plans in which a group might work together in a fairly concentrated way. First is a proposed plan of action for a day workshop, then for a weekend together, which would obviously allow for more flexible timing.

1. A ONE-DAY WORKSHOP

Purpose and structure

Aim for the day: to consider together different aspects of our unity in Christ and those attitudes which spoil it. Then to work out together a piece of dance drama on the same theme, to be incorporated into a Sunday service.

Timing: 10.00 a.m.–6.00 p.m.

Number of people: ten–twenty.

Outline programme: (this can be very flexible according to the nature of the group).

Suggested timetable

10.00 a.m.–11.00 a.m.: Introduction to day's activities.

Group Bible study. The passage may be prescribed by whoever is going to preach the sermon in the church service or, if not geared to an actual service, could be John 17:20–26 (part of Christ's prayer for the unity of his followers) or Ephesians 2:11–18 (Paul's teaching on the unity which Christ has brought through his death for us). It is necessary for the leader to have done some preparation on the passage and to introduce it in its context.

Possible questions for discussion:

(a) John 17:20–26

(i) Jesus prays that his followers "may be one" in the same way as he and his father are one. What does this mean and what are its implications in our own church life?

(ii) What is the link between believers being "perfectly one" (v. 23) and the world knowing of God and his love?

(iii) In what ways does love encourage unity?

(b) Ephesians 2:11–18

Discuss first the differences between Jews and Gentiles and the religious and cultural barriers involved.

(i) vv. 14–16. How can we, in situations of conflict, know and experience Christ to be "our peace"? Give examples, if possible.

(ii) A building is a united structure (v. 21). How can we, in our local situation, strengthen our fellowship in such ways that a "holy temple" grows up?

(iii) How can our relationships become closer to being "members of God's household"?

Encourage specific rather than generalised discussion so that people become clearer as to what they are working towards in their relationships. It is more constructive and responsible to think in terms of *my* reactions, *our* shortcomings, than of *yours* and *theirs*! Encourage the group to assume personal responsibility for their own attitudes, thinking, behaviour. Also allow time for reflection, prayer, singing together. Genuine expressions of unity and fellowship usually have humble origins when Christians are willing to become lovingly committed to each other, working out together the implications of sharing and mutuality.

Group song to learn: "We are one in the Spirit, we are one in the Lord" (no. 130, *Renewal Songbook*).

11.00 a.m.–11.30 a.m.: Break for coffee.

11.30 a.m.–12.45 p.m.: Movement work together.

This should comprise some basic movement and limbering exercises, also some dramatic improvisation (see chapter 3). Included in this could be some experimenting in portraying some of the negative attitudes which destroy unity—for example, anger, fear, jealousy and pride. Try first to 'statue' these words, then to depict them in a sequence of movement, then in a group. Encourage discussion of these attitudes—different people will express anger in different ways, verbally and physically, with much movement or with little. Some might crouch low in expressing fear, or flatten their bodies against a wall. Use different levels and body postures and talk with each other about the varied responses, otherwise people might strike a rather posed 'angry' posture without having thought-through sufficiently carefully how their own particular bodies, faces, voices react when angry.

12.45 p.m.–2.15 p.m.: Break for lunch/walk/conversation.

2.15 p.m.–4.30 p.m.: Work together on the dance drama.

This might be introduced by prayer for the church service (if the dance is to be used there) and by asking God's guidance in the out-working. The Holy Spirit is active in creativity and prayer should be consciously incorporated into this kind of working together.

One way of working is to start with a clean slate and, through discussion and experiment, to come to agreement about the content and form it will take. Another way is to start with a script or a basic idea and to work on that, modifying it as you go along and allowing group members to express ideas, suggestions, improvements. Part of the task of the group will be to learn to evaluate and sift each other's contributions, and differences arising from this can be a valid and usable part of the group's learning to work together.

A dance drama on Christian unity

Here is a suggested outline for a movement presentation on Christian unity.

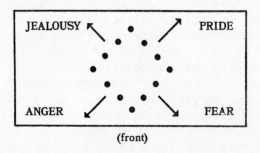

(front)

Cast: Nineteen dancers allowed for, but this can be easily modified.
    Fear group—seven
    Anger group—four
    Jealousy group—three
    Pride group—four
    Jesus

Movement:

(1) To start with, the whole group kneel in a circle, facing outwards, clasping hands with alternate people behind their backs.

(a) Cymbal clash. Anger group move quickly Down Stage Right (DSR = the performers' right-hand side) and hold a group position of anger. The rest of the group left in the circle point to Anger group, shouting "Anger!"

(b) Cymbal clash. Pride group move Up Stage Left (USL = the performers' left-hand side) and hold a position of pride, their backs turned to the rest of the group. Others again point and shout "Pride!"

(c) Cymbal clash. Jealousy group move USR and hold position of jealousy. Others point, shouting "Jealousy!"

(d) Cymbal clash. Fear group move DSL, positioning fear. Others shout "Fear!"

The dancers are now in four groups, one in each corner, holding a position that depicts the character of their word.

(2)

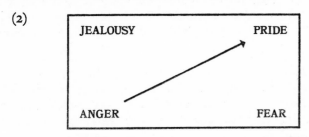

One of the Anger group rushes across towards the Pride group, raises his fist and shouts "Pride!" He beckons to the rest of his group who follow, shouting "Pride, Pride, Pride!" and all assume a menacing, angry position.

(3)

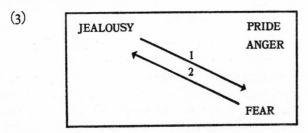

The Jealousy group move towards Fear, closely grouped, with sinister movements, saying in loud whispers "Jealousy, Jealousy, Jealousy!" As they reach the Fear group, they overpower them and Fear cower back in retreat. Then Fear rise tentatively as if appealing, but again Jealousy overpower them. Again Fear cower to the ground, huddling together in a group. Jealousy group retire to their own corner whilst everyone else repeats the word "Jealousy" several times. Fear remain on the floor.

(4)

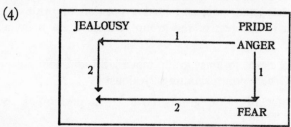

Anger group divide, half approaching Jealousy group to torment them, the other half moving towards Fear with menacing gestures. All shout "Anger, Anger, Anger!" They then return to their place DSR with slow, stamping steps and take up an angry posture.

(5) At this point Jesus begins walking up the centre aisle (of the church or hall), slowly and quietly. Fear group see him first and they reach out appealing hands to him, some quickly, others with apprehension. Jesus takes them by the hand and links them together in unity.

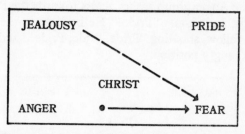

(6) As Christ encourages Fear group together, Jealousy rush over to see what is happening. Fear cower at the sight of Jealousy and Jesus turns away in sorrow and weeps. He then turns back and begins to join Jealousy together with Fear. These two groups draw gradually closer to Christ and so to each other.

(7) Christ then turns to look at the Anger group and walks towards them. He stretches out his hand to touch one of them,

their eyes meet and the angry person begins to soften. Gradually the rest of the group join hands with Jesus and lift them, linked together.

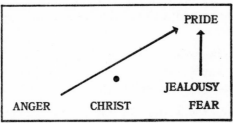

(8) All three groups now turn towards Pride group and beseech Jesus to help them. They make a pathway for Jesus to walk to Pride and raise their hands beseechingly to Pride. Then they take up different positions of encouragement, wanting Pride to join them. Christ walks to them touching first one then another until all but one bow in submission at Jesus's feet. This one continues in a proud, defiant attitude, the rest look on sadly then again raise their hands as though beseeching Pride more earnestly. The one left raises a fist high in the air but Christ lovingly reaches out until this one too kneels in penitence. All then look down or kneel down in submission to Christ.

(9) Christ now walks to each person, holding his hands over each head to bless. As he passes each, so hands are linked together in unity and fellowship. The barriers which previously divided are now broken down.

(10) Dance of joy. (Danced to "We are one in the Spirit", sung by dancers.)

Line 1 phrase 1—dancers, still with hands linked, kneel in a circle, facing inwards. Using both arms and letting go hands, describe a circular movement from the ground, crossing the arms across the body and opening them high up into the air, stretching in praise to God, then arms down to each side.

Line 1 phrase 2—repeat the former movement but, as the circle is made with the hands, the group stand and turn sideways to face a partner.

Line 2 phrase 1—using left arm and facing partner, sweep in a circular movement across body, up overhead and down to left side.

Line 2 phrase 2—repeat the above but with right arm, up and over to the right side.

Line 3 phrase 1—face into circle again, move two small steps in, reach down to ground with hands and lift them high into the air, palms uppermost.

Line 3 phrase 2—remaining in circle with arms raised, each person clasps hands with the next but one person on either side, giving the effect of a close, united group. Hands are high in the air.

Refrain line 1—still with hands in the air, the circle of people moves anti-clockwise, crossing left foot in front of right foot, step to side on right foot, cross left foot behind right foot, etc.

Refrain line 2—dancers move to form two lines, holding hands to move down centre aisle. Christ stays in the centre, watching.

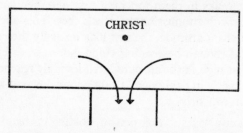

During verse two all move in two lines down the aisle to the back of the church. (If the aisle is very short, they could face inwards to each other, continuing singing the rest of the verse and refrain.)

During verse three, dancers walk back to the front and, with backs to the congregation, take up different positions of praise and worship, some kneeling, some standing, some sitting with hands lifted in thanks and adoration. The person taking the part of Christ could also join them, now becoming one of the worshipping group.

The outworking of this theme should be interspersed with discussion, perhaps exploring further the negative attitudes depicted or the ways in which Christ unites the divisions, or different ways to express worship and adoration.

4.30 p.m.–5.00 p.m.: Break for tea.

The remainder of the time could be used in different ways:

a complete run through the finished drama, discussion, a short meditation on unity, prayer.

2. A WEEKEND WORKSHOP

There might be a drama group in the church already which would benefit from a weekend away together, or perhaps a group of young people from several local churches might be invited who would like to work together on a project like this.

Purpose and structure

Aim for the weekend: to explore the theme of Christ's love for us which shows us how to love each other.
Timing: Friday evening–Sunday afternoon.
Number of people: fifteen–twenty.

Suggested timetable

Friday evening:
Supper.
Leisurely introductions if the group do not already know each other.
Meditation and discussion on John 15:12–17, Christ's command to us to love one another.

Saturday:
9.30 a.m.–10.45 a.m.: Bible study and prayer, possibly in two or three groups, on 1 John 3:11–18.

Possible questions for discussion:
(i) What does it mean "to lay down our lives for the brethren"? (v. 16).
(ii) How are we prone to "close one's heart against one's brother"?
(iii) What new ways can we discover in our local fellowship of loving in "deed and truth" rather than "word or speech"? (v. 18).

11.15 a.m.–1.00 p.m.: Basic movement, limbering, dramatic improvisation exercises.

2.00 p.m.–4.00 p.m.: Free time.

4.00 p.m.–6.00 p.m.: Start working out a piece of dance drama on the theme. Again, this can either be discussed and worked out on the spot, or a script, written previously, can be used, with the group members' own modifications and ideas being discussed and incorporated. Whatever method of production is being used (which will partly depend on whether or not a service of public portrayal is in mind), it is important that the work done becomes the group's own thinking and offering, closely related to their present learning, discussion, relating and praying. It is just possible to work on a well-prepared, polished script yet for those taking part to be minimally affected and their attitudes to remain virtually unchanged. This would say very little for dance drama as a means of learning which it most effectively can be.

"Herein is Love": an enacted meditation

Here is a scripted idea for an 'enacted meditation' with plenty of opportunity for revision and modification. The music suggested could be taped beforehand, or different music might be used. If the group were sufficiently numerous, they could perform or even compose their own music.

Cast: Jesus   The poor
       Disciples   Narrator
       Those invited to feast

(a) *Jesus and his disciples*

Introductory music: Adagio from Concerto in D Minor for two violins by Bach.

Jesus enters with a group of his disciples who gather around him, as if they are being taught.

Fade music somewhat as a narrator reads out the "I am" statements of Christ.

NARRATOR:

(i) I am from above (John 8:23).

(ii) I am in the Father and the Father in me (John 14:11).

(iii) I am the Son of God (John 10:36).

(iv) I am not alone (John 8:29).

(As the NARRATOR continues, individual disciples can make gestures of love and affection to Jesus in response to the various statements.)

    (v) I am the light of the world (John 8:12).

    (vi) I am the good shepherd (John 10:11).

    (vii) I am the door; if anyone enters by me, he will be saved, and will go in and out and find pasture (John 10:9).

    (viii) I am the way, and the truth, and the life (John 14:6).

    (ix) I am the living bread which came down from heaven; if anyone eats of this bread, he will live for ever (John 6:51).

DISCIPLE:

"Blessed is he who shall eat bread in the Kingdom of God" (Luke 14:15). Music ends.

(b) *Jesus's invitation to his feast*

NARRATOR reads the parable of the great banquet, Luke 14:16–20.

Three small groups of people enter and go to three separate positions. Each appears to be an 'in-group', exclusively concerned with its own affairs. Each is meant to characterise one of the attitudes described in the narrative.

Group 1—preoccupied with their own work.

Group 2—preoccupied with their own possessions.

Group 3—preoccupied with each other.

Jesus then sends out his disciples with invitations to a feast. As a group they walk round in a large circle, as though going out on a journey, whilst saying together the word "banquet" eight times. The walking then changes to sixteen short running steps, to the words "get ready" (eight times), again spoken together. The short steps then change to sixteen long running steps, to the words "you're invited!" (eight times) spoken with anticipation by the group.

At a cymbal clash the disciples move towards each group in turn, as though with an invitation. Some say "Come". Others gesture towards Christ's feast. But the invitation is ignored, for each group is engrossed in its own affairs. The disciples return sadly to Jesus and the three groups move off in the opposite directions and remain to one side. The mission has been in vain and the invitation ignored. The disciples gather around Jesus in disappointment.

NARRATOR reads Luke 14:21–23.

During the reading fade up part of the Adagio from Symphony in C Minor by Saint-Saëns. There enter from each side people who are poor, needy, lame, blind. The disciples are urged by Jesus to go and invite these people to the feast. Helped by the disciples, they slowly and painfully make their way towards the centre and, once there, they see Jesus and react in different ways to him. Some are fearful, others hopeful, some delighted, others timid. All recognise in him someone who can help them.

(c) *Jesus's forgiveness and healing*
NARRATOR reads extracts from "Sin" (*Prayers of Life*, Michel Quoist, pp. 105–106).

The group of needy people quietly say words like "pain", "unclean", "separation", etc.

NARRATOR: "Come unto me all you who labour and are heavy laden and I will give you rest."

Slowly and tentatively they approach Jesus who encourages them to draw near to him, to look at him, to stretch out for healing. Gradually they show each other with joy and wonder how their fears and sicknesses are healed. Then their gaze returns to Jesus and together in love, and worship, they sing together "Jesus, I love you"—verse 1 and chorus (*Songs of Fellowship*, Fountain Trust).

The three 'in-groups', who have until now kept their backs to all that has gone on, now move into a more central position; still in three groups and saying in low, avaricious tones, "Mine! mine! mine! mine!" etc. As their attention is drawn by Jesus, his disciples and the now joyful group, some, gradually seeing their own need, decide to leave their in-groups and approach Jesus for forgiveness. Others cast a scornful glance but, preferring their own pre-occupations, defiantly leave.

Fade up soft music: "He shall feed his flock" (*Messiah*, Handel). Jesus slowly moves amongst the group around him ministering to them in different ways by a look, a touch, words. Fade down the music.

The group sings together verses two and three of "Jesus, I love you".

NARRATOR: "Beloved, if God so loved us, we ought also to love one another. He who loves God should love his brother also."

Jesus now moves out of his part into the wider group who move freely around the room, affirming one another. This can be done as each chooses—an embrace or one person telling another what quality, gift, grace, characteristic he sees in him which is appreciated (e.g. "John, I'd like to thank you for being such an encouraging person." "Jane, I'd like to thank you for your real sense of humour." "Mick, I'd like to thank you for what you said in the Bible study group this morning. I found it so helpful.")

After a few minutes, when people have had time to circulate and affirm each other,

NARRATOR: "See what love the Father has given us, that we should be called children of God, and so we are. Beloved, we are God's children now; it does not yet appear what we shall be, but we know that when he appears we shall be like him, for we shall see him as he is." (1 John 3:12)

The whole group now join in an act of praise and worship, singing "Allelujah" (*Sound of Living Waters*, Hodder and Stoughton). The whole thing could finish with prayer or time for silent adoration of God.

Production notes: (a) The 'preoccupied groups' should have the opportunity to discuss their preoccupations thoroughly, and the personal implications of them (e.g. "How can such preoccupations assume a wrong priority so that we are missing out on more important things?"). They could also work at their piece of mime/movement on their own and experiment with portraying their particular piece. A difficulty might well arise over some of the group's having to 'reject' the invitation to the feast, since this will deny them joining in the affirming and the loving and worshipping group at the end and might leave some feeling depressed and excluded. One possibility is that, in time, all repent of their preoccupations and come to Jesus. But this might appear to be a denial of the truth that some people will, by virtue of their own choices in life, exclude themselves from the enjoyment of Christ's company. Another is that just before the mutual affirmations, *everyone* moves out of role, Jesus as well, and as themselves, affirm, sing and worship God together.

(b) The 'needy group' should discuss their reactions at being invited to such a feast. Since the suggested ending is an interpretation rather than part of the recorded parable, take time to consider its suitability.

(c) Take time to explain the extempore affirming which will take place. Discuss it, and the place there is amongst us for mutual encouragement and recognition. Our tendency is to criticise each other negatively rather than make a practice of saying what we appreciate in each other! It is best not to rehearse this, for it is in no way an act but something deeply meaningful. Discuss how, by finding ways of affirming each other in daily life, we are obeying Christ's command to love each other.

(d) Let the 'disciples group' discuss things like their relationship to Jesus, their feelings as the invitation to the feast is rejected, their attitudes to helping the needy to the feast.

(e) Songs and readings can usefully be rehearsed separately as well as together with the movement. People will feel more free in worship if they know the songs well and have learnt the words, all of which are fairly simple and easy to learn.

(f) It is also helpful, at some stage, to discuss the parable of the feast in terms of love for Christ, love for others, love of self, priorities of love. Much useful teaching and learning could emerge through honest sharing.

8.00 p.m.–10.00 p.m.: Continue work on different parts, including prayer together, singing, discussion and, of course, movement.

Sunday
9.30 a.m.–10.45 a.m.: Group Bible study and prayer on 1 John 4:13–21.

Possible questions for discussion:

(i) What is the full meaning of "confessing that Jesus is the Son of God"? (v. 15).

(ii) "There is no fear in love" (v. 18). What are some of our fears and how can we discover that "perfect love casts out fear"?

(iii) Use vv. 20, 21 as the basis for private self-examination and confession. How can we help each other towards replacing 'hating' relationships by 'loving' ones?

11.30 a.m.–1.00 p.m.: Limbering exercises, movement and improvisation. Finish working on the dance drama.

2.00 p.m.–3.00 p.m.: Either free time (if people do not need to depart early) or (if an early finish is necessary) put the whole thing together as an act of worship, perhaps also incorporating more singing or instrumental music, poems or meditations or readings from group members.

Either before going home or, if all from the same church, the following week, meet together to de-brief the weekend in order to discover its value and what people learnt from working together in this way. Obviously these are only two examples of how a group could usefully spend time together working on dance drama. If an immediate goal (e.g. a church service) is in mind there is usually real incentive to work hard and share ideas. If the group can also experience a close integration of movement, Bible reading, discussion, prayer and sharing, there will be opportunities for them to learn at different levels. Often, out of such learning experiences can come significant Christian insights and personal development.

It might occasionally be possible to organise a workshop lasting several days. We have experimented with a five days' creativity workshop for about forty people on the subject of personal freedom. During that time the three areas of dance drama, music and art were available as means of exploring the liberty given to God's children. Each morning began with small group Bible studies along this theme and the rest of the day was devoted to practical work in the particular media chosen. Each person opted for two out of three areas. A dance drama called "Freedom Maker", depicting different scenes from Christ's ministry, was worked out, an original setting of the Genesis Creation story was written by the music group, whilst the artists painted, carved, made collages and hessian banners. The climax of the workshop was a two-hour festival of praise and worship where the different activities were brought together in a most moving celebration of God's love to his people and their love for one another. Many of the course members had rarely or never participated in these sorts of artistic activities and the quality of work produced was a powerful testimony to the creative, liberating work of the Holy Spirit.

CHAPTER 7

Dance in Praise and Prayer

1. Body Posture in Prayer

'HANDS TOGETHER, EYES closed'—goes the formula. And in thinking about posture in prayer we tend to refer to a certain limited range of positions such as kneeling down with hands held palms together or covering the face. Standing up, the head is normally bowed in reverence, perhaps with the hands clasped in front of the body. Or, in some traditions, the praying congregation remain seated with shoulders leaning forwards and head bowed. As we watch the vicar kneeling in prayer, his body is normally passive, in a position of reverence and submission, yet his mind and spirit are active, reaching out to God. For some, the bodily attitude of prayer can be problematic. If the muscles are tense and agitated or lethargic and weary then the spirit has difficulty in becoming composed. If there is insufficient air in the room or the person cannot find a comfortable position, again, prayer is more difficult. Most of us experience some degree of struggle between the spirit and the body which will either find a resolution or cause us to give up temporarily in favour of something else.

Our bodies are an important part of us and we cannot simply 'put them aside' in prayer. Breathing exercises can help us to relax and, by experimenting, we can discover a bodily position in which we are relaxed—though not to the point of falling asleep! Prayer is not limited to the spirit or mind—we pray through our bodies and our praying should be an activity of our whole person, body, mind and spirit. We talk about 'praying with our whole being' but often do not work this out in reality. Some Christian ascetics have tried to discipline and starve their bodies rigorously so that they might cultivate the life of the spirit. The danger here, if carried to excess, is a wrong denial of the body, whereas the Bible teaches that the whole person—including his body—is the dwelling place of God's Spirit. Paul teaches the Corinthian Christians that their bodies "are members of Christ", "temple(s) of the Holy Spirit within you". "You are not your own; you were bought with a price. So glorify God in your body" (1 Corinthians 6:15, 19, 20).

Sometimes we experience a close correspondence between body and spirit. Perhaps it happens when both are still and quiet before God. Or, as we are particularly aware of God's holiness, our spirits and our bodies may be prostrate before him. As we intercede for others, helping them to bear their burdens, we may 'square our shoulders' on their behalf. When we grieve or sorrow in prayer our bodies may correspond by weeping. I have even known someone, praying with great joy, to laugh in such a way that it was not an intrusion into his praying but part of it! So our bodies are not passive or redundant in prayer but caught up into it by the Holy Spirit. André Louf writes: "Every prayer, however secret and however interior it may be, will be mirrored in the body. Prayer cannot happen without the body, either with beginners or with those who are advanced in prayer. Gradually, prayer and the Spirit take possession of the body. Body and Spirit are bound up inseparably together."[1]

To what extent are our bodies restricted to positions of stillness in prayer? If we want to rejoice in God and the spirit of praise surges up within us, must our bodies remain passive? Joy and praise find different expressions at different times. There is that quiet, peaceful joy when God's Spirit seems to wash over ours and we are content to be still before him. There is also the joyful praise which wells up in us making our bodies as well as our spirits want to soar.

Just as dance and movement featured in ancient Israel's praise and worship, so they find a place in other cultures and religious groups. Vigorous dancing in praise of God is a marked and colourful feature of the Black Pentecostal Churches in the U.S.A. and also in the Chilean Pentecostal Churches. Professor W. J. Hollenweger describes his experience during a church service in Chile:

The writer was asked to sit in front of the congregation in the red plush seat reserved for honoured guests. An ocean of faces floated before my eyes, two thousand to three thousand faithful, some with car tyres on their feet instead of shoes. But as soon as the trumpet blew the first melody, those faces, creased with the signs of age-long oppression, came to life. In a circle the people danced slowly the dances of their Indian ancestors. Those who did not dance stood reverently and clapped their hands slowly. A woman prophesied in a deep, soul-searching voice. All of a sudden there was silence! The whole congregation fell down on their knees in order to thank God for the dance he had given them . . . "Do you also dance?" they asked me. This was the test-question. They wanted to know whether I despised them or not. "I would like to," I answered sincerely, "but I do not know your dances." They were satisfied with this answer. Their own preachers often do not dance either; their duty is not to dance, but to interpret the dances.[2]

This kind of worship might seem very strange to some, provoking opinions such as 'emotional', 'embarrassing', 'hysterical', 'out of control', etc. British people are undemonstrative and reserved and many would feel that a happening such as this sounds more like an entertainment than church worship. Professor Hollenweger stresses that the dancing was in no way uncontrolled. He writes: "The nearest parallel with which I could compare it is a really skilful pianist who knows the technique of keyboard playing. The skill is a matter of many years of practice and exercise. The way in which he uses it is a matter of the inspiration of the moment." This principle of control is important. Dancing is a feature of many cults and religions. Where it degenerates into a hysterical frenzy where the participants are out of control, then it would seem manifestly clear that this is not inspired by the Holy Spirit. In any true spiritual manifestation, Paul teaches, "the spirits of the prophets are subject to prophets. For God is not a God of confusion but of peace" (1 Corinthians 14:32, 33). Self-control and order are the biblical criteria of any spontaneous manifestations of the Holy Spirit in church worship.

In addition to groups which have, for some years, been encouraging liturgical dance and religious drama, there has also been a resurgence of both in many churches affected by the charismatic renewal movement. Encouraged by groups such as Shekinah, the Fisherfolk and the Sacred Dance Group, dances of praise and thanksgiving have increasingly become a feature of church services, "Glory in the Church" festivals, central rallies and weekend workshops. Some of these are presentations whilst others, with accompanying songs, are worshipful acts of joy and praise in which the body as well as the voice makes its glad response to God. Much of our church worship has become very 'pew bound' yet, to some who like an ordered service, such innovations may cause anxiety. Bearing in mind the principle of self-control and order, what can be said in favour of some people (if not all) dancing as well as singing the praises of God?

Firstly, if well done, such dancing is a vehicle of praise, joy and thanksgiving offered to God. Our bodies can unite with our minds and spirits in glorifying our Creator. Secondly, we can discover, through dance, new degrees of personal liberty and freedom. Partly this comes through a willingness to learn simple steps and movements, but also, as we allow God's Spirit increasing access to every part of our person, those areas of us which were once confused, hidden, self-conscious and fearful, become healed, re-owned and free to praise God. Christ promised, "If the Son sets you free, you will indeed be free." For some this may mean freedom from specific sins, for others freedom from some of the consequences of sin, such as self-consciousness, inferiority, or distaste for their own bodies. This personal freedom is to be realised and received and allowed to grow in us, not for selfish use, but so that we might be the more available to God and the service of other people. One sure indication that we are increasing in Christian freedom will be our growing desire to praise and worship him with our whole being. For some, this can include dance. Thirdly, our expression of love for God can be extended by using our bodies as vehicles of praise. The language of love is wonderfully varied. We can tell God we love him by using words, by singing, by the wordless lift of our spirits, by the held look of love and adoration. We can also love him with our bodily movements and gestures.

Used with Christian integrity, these are some of the ways in which dance can promote God's praise in worship. In some churches affected by charismatic renewal, group and individual dance has been included in services with the congregation either watching or singing. This is no gimmick but, properly used, is part of that living flexibility which the Spirit is bringing to some of our liturgical forms and traditions.

> Fill *every part* of me with praise;
> Let *all my being* speak
> Of Thee and of Thy love, O Lord!
> Poor though I be, and weak.

In the remainder of this chapter, we shall outline first some dances of praise and worship set to fairly well-known songs, with the hope that they will provide ideas which can then be extended to other songs and music. Secondly, there are other suggestions as to how movement can be used in other acts of prayer, both private and public.

2. PRAISE AND THANKSGIVING

These dances are not intended for a whole congregation but could well be used in church worship with a group of dancers and either a group of singers or, if the songs are known more generally, with the congregation singing the words. References to words and music are taken from the song book, *Sound of Living Waters* by Betty Pulkingham and Jeanne Harper (Hodder and Stoughton, 1974).

(a) "*Alleluia*" (*Sound of Living Waters*, p. 49)

Here is a beautiful and simple song of adoration to Christ. It could be used by a group in a church service or workshop, or by an individual in private prayer. For each verse work out four (or eight) very simple movements which seem to you to match the words. Here are a few suggestions to experiment with and then arrange and extend as you choose. If used by a group, they could stand in a circle, or a semi-circle with their backs facing the congregation. (i) With the palm of the right hand facing you and the fingers together, slowly stretch up the right arm until extended, letting the eyes and neck follow in the same direction. (ii) Make a similar movement with the left hand and arm. (iii) Slowly lower the arms to each side as far as shoulder level, so that they are extended to the right and left, palms uppermost. (iv) Slowly close the arms in to chest level, bending the elbows and bringing the hands together, palms gently cupped upwards as though making an offering. Now try a similar sequence in a kneeling position.

Experiment with other arm movements expressing adoration, e.g. stretch the arms high above the head with the backs of the hands facing the body and the palms uppermost. Gently move them from right to left in a slow 'waving' movement. Or try large circular movements, sweeping the right arm slowly across the body, clockwise with the back of the hand facing the body and circling it round back to the right side of the body. Try this circular sweeping with both arms, either with both arms moving in a clockwise circle or with right arm moving clockwise and the left arm anti-clockwise across the body. Now, kneeling down, circles can be described similarly with the arms, this time on a different plane, the right arm moving from the body at chest level outwards and clockwise so that the arm is extended, palm uppermost, still at chest level. Other simple movements can be worked out either from a standing position or kneeling on one or both knees. Keep the movements simple, slow and reverent.

(b) "*Father, we adore you*" (*Sound of Living Waters*, p. 49)

Here is another song of adoration to which a dance can be set. The dancers should stand either in small circles of four or in one large circle, facing inwards, arms by sides, feet slightly apart.

	Bars	*Movement*
Verse 1	1–2	Slowly stretch up both arms, palms uppermost, backs of hands facing the floor. Lift eyes and head also.
	3–4	Bring down arms each side to shoulder level, keeping them extended and with palms uppermost so that each person is lightly touching, but not holding, the hands of the next person in the circle. At the same

	Bars	Movement
		time, the group walks round four steps, clockwise, leading with the right foot on the word 'lay'. Keep eyes and head up.
	5–6	Facing into the centre, draw extended arms in to chest-level, bending the elbows and cupping the hands, wrists together with fingers curving upwards like a flask. On 'we' step back with left foot and on 'love', kneel on to the right knee and stretch up the cupped hands as though making an offering.
Verse 2	1–2	From kneeling position, slowly stand, stretching up the arms and hands, palms uppermost, as in verse 1. Follow through the same sequence for the rest of verse 2 and verse 3.

(c) "Alleluia", No. 1 (Sound of Living Waters, p. 12)

This is a song of praise and thanksgiving with a beautiful rhythm. The dance set to it is for six dancers. They begin in a circle, arms by sides, hands joined and feet slightly apart.

	Bars	Movement
Chorus 1	1–2	Sway to right, sway to left.
	3–4	Repeat, raising hands slowly so that they are fully up on 'Lord'.
	5–6	Repeat with hands fully raised.
	7–8	Step back with right foot on 'praise', close with left foot on 'name', lowering hands.
Verse 1	1–2	Drop hands, turn and extend right arm to centre of circle. Take two side steps to centre (right foot leading), joining hands and raising them on 'Lord'.
	3–4	Two small side steps left (away from centre) with right hands still joined. Left hands sweep out sideways with head movement following.

	Bars	*Movement*
	5–6	Release right hands and repeat bars 1–2, hands raised at the centre with palms facing body.
	7–8	Step back on left foot, close with right foot. Repeat. The left arm is extended sideways. To re-form the wide circle, face centre and join hands at arm's length.
Chorus 2	1–2	Drop hands, sway right slightly bending right leg and sweeping left arm in a circular movement across body and over head, anti-clockwise with the back of the left hand leading. Repeat movement to the left using right arm.
	3–4	With hands held palms up at chest level, step back on to right foot on 'thanks'. Kneel on left knee on 'risen' with hands held palms up at left knee level. Look up.
	5–6	Quickly stand and repeat bars 1–2, to left first then to right.
	7–8	Left foot forward on 'praise', close with right foot. Hands palms up at waist level then raise them fully on 'name'.
Verse 2	1–2	Left hands drop to side. Right hands join in centre. Take two small step-close steps in to centre, right foot leading.
	3–4	Two small step-close steps away from centre, left foot leading, sweeping both arms out in a throwing movement.
	5–6	Two step-close steps turning to face centre, head bowed and arms sweeping round to centre. Right hands are joined and left hands just beneath them.
	7–8	On 'risen', raise left arm up, palm uppermost, over head and out to side. Right hands remain joined. Right foot remains fixed. Straighten left leg and with left foot describe an arc to the left. The circle is now facing in a clockwise direction.
Chorus 3	1–2	Still facing clockwise, on the spot sway right moving left arm as in chorus 2. Step forward with left foot (in clockwise direction), swaying left and moving right arm as before.
	3–4	As chorus 2, but stepping forward in a clockwise direction with right foot.

	Bars	Movement
	5–6	As chorus 2, but stepping forward clockwise with left foot and right arm, then right foot and left arm.
	7–8	Still facing clockwise, as in chorus 2.
Verse 3	1–4	Right hands joined at centre of circle. Left arms extended, still in clockwise direction with heads bowed on to them (bar 1). Then three chassé steps, left foot leading, beginning on 'cruc. . . .' (bars 2–4).
	5–6	One more chassé. Step towards centre of circle with right foot, raising hands quickly on 'live'.
	7–8	Step back with right foot and close left foot (twice), bringing hands down and joining in a wide circle.
Chorus 4		As chorus 2.
		(Verse 4 not used.)
Verse 5	1–2	Still in a circle, form three couples (turning to the person next to you). Face each other. Move towards partner with two chassé steps, right foot leading, right palms meeting and raised together on 'praise'.
	3–4	Pass partner and move towards next contrary partner, left foot leading and left hands held at waist level.
	5–6	Repeat bars 1–2 with next contrary partner. Form a circle, holding hands, those travelling clockwise facing outwards, those counter-clockwise facing in.
Chorus 5	1–6	As Chorus 1, but in the positions of verse 5 end.
	7–8	Hands separated and lowered to outward stretch to congregation, those facing in turning on right shoulder to face outwards.
Chorus 6	1–6	Hands down, join quickly and repeat chorus 5.
	7–8	Hands separated and lowered to outward stretch to congregation, palms up, crossing neighbours' hands at wrists, left hands under right hands.

(d) "I am the bread of life" (Sound of Living Waters, p. 110)

This song, which could aptly be used within the context of a Communion service, celebrates the resurrection of Christ and the subsequent resurrection of the believer. The accompanying movement introduces some mime. It is for six dancers who begin in the form of a cross.

```
            *
        ×   ×   ×
            o
            +
```

× * stand, o kneeling upright on one knee. + kneels, sitting on heels. Heads are bowed, hands behind backs.

	Bars	Movement
Verse 1	1–2	Raise head, bring hands to chest on 'I'. Arms stretched out in front in a giving gesture on 'life', palms up.
	3–4	Draw hands back to chest, palms up. Extend arms forward, hands side by side and cupped on 'hunger'.
	5–6	Hands together, as in prayer, at chin level (not too close to body). Arms extended forward, right hand on top of left on 'thirst'.
	7–8	Dancers * × o + bring their outstretched arms down to each side, palms facing their bodies and heads bowed. The two side dancers × bring both arms to one side of the body, away from the centre.
	9–10	Left hand dropped to side, right hand raised quickly, palm facing the body, and slowly lowered, bending at elbow, to shoulder level, head following. On 'draw him' × kneel on right knee, * remains standing. All bow heads.
Chorus 1	1–2	Arms raised slowly, outstretched at each side with palms up, to shoulder level on 'up', head following movement. + rises to upright kneeling position.
	3–4	Arms raised to be fully up on 'up'. ×o+ all stand.
	5–8	Take four steps (one per bar) turning on right shoulder round and back to the front, arms still raised, falling slowly on 'last day', as o+ resume original positions.
Verse 2	1–2	Right hand makes a 'giving' gesture (like scattering seed from a basket) on 'bread', the left hand similarly on 'give'. So both are extended to the congregation.
	3–4	Cross arms on chest on 'flesh', draw them down then raise them at each side, palms up, on 'world', to just below shoulder level.

	Bars	Movement
	5–6	Hands side by side, palms facing body, at mouth level then draw down to chest level.
	7–8	Arms drawn back for cymbal-type clap (soundless) at chin level on 'live', hands continuing up to top of head then drawn down to shoulder level.
	9–10	Repeat bars 7–8, but 'clap' to full stretch up then draw down to sides. × kneel on right knee on 'ever'.
Chorus 2		As chorus 1.
Verse 3	1–2	As verse 2, bars 5–6.
	3–4	Arms crossed on chest on 'flesh', head bowed on 'man'.
	5–6	Hands held cupped, right on top of left, a little way from the body at chest level.
	7–8	As 5–6, raising 'cup' to mouth level, with head movement following.
	9–10	Arms down and crossed in front of the body, sweeping out to either side, palms facing body, in a 'cancelling' action, head bowed. × kneel on right knee on 'in you'.
Chorus 3		As chorus 1.
Verse 4	1–2	Slowly raise arms, palms uppermost, from hip to shoulder level in front with elbows bent, head movement following.
	3–4	'Giving' gesture with both hands, palms up.
	5–6	'Praying' gesture, hands together at chin level.
	7–8	Right hand on chest with right arm held horizontal with head bowed on to it. Left arm down by side.
	9–10	As verse 2, bars 9–10. × kneel on right knee on 'ever'.
Chorus 4		As chorus 1, but moving into a semi-circle and joining hands on 'last day'.
		× *
		× ×
		o +
Verse 5	1–2	Hands joined, move to 'praying' position on 'believe'.
	3–4	Elbows bent, hands at face level, palms almost facing each other.
	5–6	Hands slowly raised in front, palms up, to just above head level, head movement following.

Bars	Movement
7–8	Hands lowered to chest level, palms up, head movement following.
9–10	Join hands in a circle.
Chorus 5 1–2	Moving clockwise in the circle with hands joined, two skip-change steps beginning with right foot. The head and body are bowed on the first step then rise until hands are at shoulder level by 'up'.
3–4	Two skip-change steps, beginning with right foot, head bowed on first step and rising as hands are raised to be fully up on 'up'.
5–8	Facing the centre of the circle, with head and body bowed and arms down on 'raise', step into centre with right foot and raise arms until fully up on 'up'. Move out of circle to face congregation in a semi-circle on 'last'. Bring arms slowly down to each side, palms up.

(A 'skip-change step', known also as a 'barn dance step' or a 'Scottish dance travelling step', is basically a four-beat step—right foot step forward, left foot close behind, right foot step forward again, hop on right foot bringing left foot through to step left foot forward, right foot close, left foot forward, hop on left foot, etc.)

Another way of interpreting this song—and especially suitable for a workshop—is to teach the steps of the chorus to everyone then let small groups work out a simple mime/movement for each verse.

(e) Other dances of praise

There are many hymns and songs of praise where dance can be used. The song book already suggested provides many excellent ones for use by groups or individuals. "Thank, thank you, Jesus" (*Sound of Living Waters*, p. 50) is a beautiful and simple expression of love to which movements might be matched, likewise the well-known "Come Together" version of "Holy, Holy" (*Sound of Living Waters*, p. 40). Using some of the basic arm and body movements suggested in the foregoing dances, the reader could now go on to work out some other dances of praise and thanksgiving. It is not only modern songs which can be used either. Some of the older, more traditional words and music can also be given dance settings, provided they are carefully worked out. Or take one of the oldest Christian hymns, the Magnificat, and try interpreting it in dance and movement. The Gelineau musical setting of it might inspire some. Another possibility is to use verses of Scripture set to music. Some, such as the "Scripture in Song" recordings, are already popular and known to many people. One of these, "The Lord Thy God in the midst of thee is mighty", from Zephaniah 3:17, could well be given matching movement. In the Psalms is a wide range of poetry of praise and thanksgiving. A group could look together at Psalm 145:10–21, a passage where David extols the character of God. Part of this might be set to music with matching dance movements. Likewise in Psalms 148, 149, 150 the praises of the writer could well overflow into music and dancing.

After the Israelites had crossed the Red Sea, Miriam, Aaron's sister, led the women in song and dance, praising God for what he had done for them. Her thanksgiving overflowed into every part of her—feet included! Doubtless there will be times when we want to respond similarly.

I have sometimes found, in times of private prayer, that the whole being—mind, spirit and body—wants to respond in thanksgiving and love to God. This might sometimes be in great stillness, when words and singing and reading are, for a time, put aside in order to love and adore in response to the outpoured grace of the Father. At other times love will want to express itself through bodily movement and dance. On those occasions I use a record or taped music in order to help me offer praise to God through movement. For some people verbal fluency and self-expression can be quite a problem. A friend once expressed personal sorrow that she found praying aloud in a fellowship group very difficult and embarrassing because of her lack of fluency with words. Then one day she asked permission to pray in tongues. This was given and with quiet joy she prayed in a fluent spiritual tongue which was then interpreted by someone else in the group. God gifts us with rich variety of expression and, for some, there may be means of expression less usual but still valid if under the control of God's

Spirit and (when offered publicly) open to the fellowship of believers.

A teacher of Physical Education who attended a Christian creativity workshop wrote afterwards:

> Praise his name that there was no competitive element . . . and that we were free to explore new methods of communication. One of my most cherished memories will be the last night when three of us just danced. I danced, I think in a way that I've never done before, a time of true worship when I felt I was giving myself and receiving from God in a truly wonderful way . . . I think that was the first time in my life that I've ever felt so liberated in dance and I just gave it to God as my own thank-offering. So often, as a teacher, one misses out on the sheer joy of 'doing' as one teaches. It was wonderful to have the opportunity to 'do' and to do for him who created us and made it possible.

3. PRAYING FOR OTHERS

It may seem far-fetched to some to suggest using dance when we pray for others. Certainly it is not the kind of activity one would expect to see in the middle of a church prayer meeting! Yet I would like to suggest that, for some who enjoy movement, it can be an aid to our personal intercessions. Most of us find there are times when our prayers for others become heavy-going and unimaginative. We know we ought to pray for Jane in Thailand but she seems so remote. Peter is depressed and low—how do we pray for him? Mrs. Brown is full of arthritis and often in pain. Do we just pray, "God, please heal Mrs. Brown. It can't be your will for her to be in such pain. Lift Peter's depression and please bless Jane"? Many of us would have to admit we only scratch the surface in our praying for others and are still beginners.

Sometimes we use aids to help us pray more imaginatively and with more immediacy. Photos, letters, the sound of a person's voice can increase our desire to pray. We could also use our bodies to identify a little more closely with others' needs. First, quietly think of that person as you come to pray for him or her—recalling physical appearance, facial expression, voice, activities, etc. Then ask God to show you, from his perspective, more about that person's needs. Avoid dashing in, thinking you know exactly what is wrong or what he needs, for often our perspective is partial only so that we pray about the top-growth rather than the roots of the matter. (e.g. Anger and resentment may be at the root of a person's depression rather than an uninteresting job.) Take whatever God seems to show you of the need, such as bodily pain, tiredness, fear, perplexity, and portray it in movement or a held pose. Try hobbling stiffly (as Mrs. Brown always does) or feeling the tension of fear. Walk round the room imagining how loneliness feels or how it feels when everyone around you is speaking a language you cannot yet understand—as happens with new missionaries. Imagine you are that person.

After a few moments, try portraying your desire and prayer for him. Perhaps you will want to smooth the painful joints and touch them as Jesus may have done. Perhaps you will want to take him by the arm and lead him from his place of fear to a place of freedom where he can look up to Jesus. You might want to sit with her in her loneliness or lay hands on her head, ears and mouth as she is involved in language-learning. You may want, through mime, to perform some ministry of love, such as wiping away tears or holding a sorrowful person. Perhaps the need is such that you do not know what to do. So now, in silence, wait upon God, first lifting that person in his presence in the simple faith that God wants to work in his life, then asking God if there is anything he wants you to do—a deed, a conversation, a letter, a phone-call. This is not the same thing as having bright ideas springing from one's own initiative. Learning to listen to God takes time and a genuine desire to discover what he is saying. It is one thing to be active in doing good (which I would in no way disparage), and another to discern God's directives, timing and ways as we learn to minister to others in his name.

It might be helpful at this point to describe a time of prayer for others which a friend and I undertook, partly through movement.

There were several people for whom we were wanting to pray —some were known to both of us, though not all. Yet all seemed to be passing through a time of personal need, either physical or emotional. So we decided to experiment by using our bodies as well as our minds and spirits to intercede. We were allowed to use the chapel of a nearby convent where we could remain uninterrupted for about two hours.

First we shared briefly with each other the needs of an individual as we understood them. Then, in silence, we each sought to interpret in movement and mime that person's need. (e.g. As we concentrated prayer on a woman troubled by fear and anxiety which restricted her daily living severely and caused her frustration, we portrayed this in movement. One 'drew' a small circle around her, trying to move around in the limited space where movements could only be angular, inturned and cramped. The other person made darting, neurotic movements within a confined space and felt the consequent frustration.) We then went on to use contrasting movements, such as helping the person to step out of her cramped circle, encouraging her to stretch her legs and arms. One of us 'became' the woman, running and jumping in new freedom. After a few moments and without discussion, each of us knelt in silence to hold her in God's presence for him to bring his healing love to her. If we felt God was saying anything to us in the silence, we quietly shared it with each other. Then, after a pause, we went on to pray for another person.

We continued praying like this for about an hour, at the end of which we were both feeling weary and drained of energy. So next we put on a record of part of the Passion music from Handel's *Messiah*. Sometimes with movement and sometimes kneeling in stillness, we focused our attention on Christ's sufferings on behalf of the world. "He was despised and rejected"; "All we like sheep have gone astray"; "The Lord hath laid on him the iniquity of us all"—some of this beautiful music led us to dance out, with reverence, our adoration of Christ. At other moments we simply remained kneeling in silent worship. The chorus swept on into "Worthy is the Lamb" and we saw our praying in the perspective of his majesty and Kingship, "for he must reign until he has put all his enemies under his feet". Joy and wonder filled us as we realised against the indestructible Lordship of Christ. We left tired but rejoicing! Looking back to that day we have seen some of God's wonderful answers to those prayers.

I am not suggesting that all our praying for others should take unusual forms like this. It is far more important to know that we are co-operating in prayer with God in the outworking of his plans for people, whatever methods we use. Yet, for me, that particular afternoon of intercession remains as something very meaningful in which I was completely involved. I know of others also who sometimes pray like this in the privacy of their own rooms, unobserved yet offering themselves in prayer for others in need. Some readers may find it worth trying.

The music I have found most helpful in this context varies in style. Sometimes a simple song, such as "Peace is flowing like a river" (*Sound of Living Waters*, p. 159), can give a lead into prayer, or Bach's "Commit thy ways to Jesus" from the *St. Matthew Passion*. Bach's organ music will, for some, be inspiring. I have also enjoyed using his Double Violin Concerto in D minor (second movement; Largo), Albinoni's Adagio for strings and orchestra and Saint-Saëns' Symphony in C minor (Adagio movement).

4. OTHER ACTS OF PRAYER

We have looked at dance as an act of praise and intercession. Finally, there are also other parts of prayer in which movement might be used. In a workshop I attended with the Sacred Dance Group, we were invited to consider some of our shortcomings and sins before God then, without discussion, to acknowledge and confess them through movement. It was salutary, in the first place, to have to consider this in a fairly specific way. Most of us probably ask God to "forgive us our sins" without being very specific as to what that particular day's sins have been. Perhaps one has been living life too fast without sufficient time for reflection, thereby bringing hurt to others and oneself. Perhaps there has been selfishness or unkind speech or a holding on to resentments. I was interested that this acting out did not breed introspection—if anything it helped one to be more objective and specific. It was not prolonged and then we were invited to leave our burdens with God and receive his forgiveness and cleansing. For some it proved a very meaningful way in to dances of praise and thanksgiving.

It also makes a good group activity to work out movements to the Lord's Prayer, perhaps using the calypso tune with the recurring line "Hallowed be Thy name". There are also parts of the Series 3 Communion Service where reverent dance would be appropriate as parts of the congregational responses, such as the Offertory or the Gloria. These would not be included as 'performances' but as the offering of one particular group of the church within the whole service. It would be helpful, in this context as in other services, for the vicar or minister to explain to the congregation that, whether through hymns, spoken responses, Bible reading, teaching, prayer or dance, every activity is part of the service of worship offered to God, rather than novelty or entertainment. In this way, people can be helped to understand better the rich variety of worship.

These, then, are some of the ways in which dance and movement can enrich our praises and praying so that, with our whole being, we can glorify our Creator.

CHAPTER 8

Four Longer Scripts

IN THIS CHAPTER we shall look at more ways of working out ideas and scripts. Most of these are longer ones, suitable for use in a church service, though they could be adapted for wider use as well. The first two are New Testament parables, the third is on the theme of Fellowship and the fourth shows how a whole anthology can be compiled to teach about the ministry of Christ.

1. THE TENANTS AND THE VINEYARD (Luke 20:9–15)

Cast: Four narrators   One vineyard owner
One drum player   Three servants
Seven people to form the vineyard   Jesus
Four tenants

One way of achieving dramatic effect is through a rhythmic use of the voice, called 'voice percussion'. In this parable we use a small chorus of people together with a drum accompaniment to emphasise the rhythm. The chorus both accompany and narrate the parable whilst the rest perform the action. Numbers could be somewhat reduced if necessary. The drum accompaniment is kept up continuously, though, as indicated in the script, the rhythm changes from time to time.

Drum and voice percussion	Action
1 2 3 4	
Drum beats (quite a brisk pace) He (solo voice)	Seven people enter to form a vineyard, backs to the audience, arms linked to make branches.
1 2 planted a vineyard	
1 2 3 Chorus (softly) vineyard, vineyard, vineyard, **4** vineyard,	The owner enters, considers the land, digs and plants, then stands back to admire it.
1 2 3 4 Drum beats He (solo voice)	He beckons to the tenants who enter, inspect the vineyard and strike a bargain with the owner.
1 2 hired it to tenants,	

Drum and voice percussion	Action
Chorus (softly) tenants, tenants, tenants, tenants,	He takes his leave of them, they wave, see him on his way then turn to admire the vineyard.

Drum and voice percussion	Action

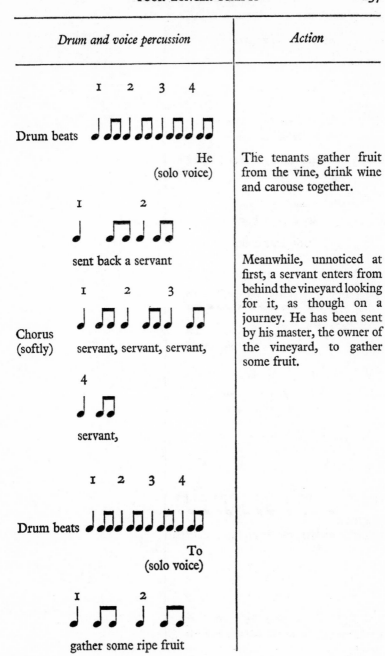

The tenants gather fruit from the vine, drink wine and carouse together.

Meanwhile, unnoticed at first, a servant enters from behind the vineyard looking for it, as though on a journey. He has been sent by his master, the owner of the vineyard, to gather some fruit.

Drum and voice percussion	Action

Chorus
(softly)   ripe fruit, ripe fruit, ripe

fruit, ripe fruit,

To
(solo voice)

bring to his master,

Chorus
(softly)   master, master, master, master,

Drum beats

Drum and voice percussion	*Action*
Chorus with drum (urgently) careful! careful! careful! careful! look! look! look! look!	The servant approaches the tenants in the vineyard. As he moves towards them, and following the voice percussion, they menace him calling out "Beat him!" (four times). He falls to his knees, shielding his face. They beat him. Painfully he pulls himself side stage and remains there.
1 2 3 4 Drum beats He (solo voice) 1 2 sent another servant 1 2 3 Chorus (softly) servant, servant, servant,	The tenants now join to dance in the vineyard. They swing around in a circle and make merry together. In the meantime, a second servant enters from behind the vineyard, as on a journey. He sees the tenants and approaches them.

Drum and voice percussion	Action

4

servant,

1   2   3   4

Drum beats

To
(solo voice)

1   2

gather some ripe fruit

1   2   3

Chorus   ripe fruit, ripe fruit, ripe
(softly)

4

fruit, ripe fruit,

1   2   3   4

Drum beats

To
(solo voice)

Drum and voice percussion	Action
1 **2** ♩ ♫ ♩ ♫ bring to his master	
1 **2** **3** **4** ♩ ♫ ♩ ♫ ♩ ♫ ♩ ♫ Chorus master, master, master, master, (softly)	
1 **2** **3** **4** Drum beats ♩ ♫ ♩ ♫ ♩ ♫ ♩	
Chorus they'll hurt you! hurt you! and drum (urgently) hurt you! hurt you! Look! look! look! look!	As he draws near, and following the voice percussion, they shout out "Kick him!" (four times). He falls in pain to the ground then pulls himself along and lies beside the first servant.
1 **2** **3** **4** Drum beats ♩ ♫ ♩ ♫ ♩ ♫ ♩ ♩ He (solo voice)	The tenants now sit or lie down, propped up against each other, to sleep. The third servant approaches from behind the vineyard, and one tenant stirs, awakens and then wakes the others.

Drum and voice percussion	Action

1   2

♩ ♫ ♩ ♫

sent a third ser-vant

1   2   3

♩ ♫ ♩ ♫ ♩ ♩

Chorus
(softly)   servant, servant, servant,

4

♩ ♫

servant,

1   2   3   4

♩ ♫ ♫ ♫ ♫ ♫ ♫ ♫

Drum beats

To
(solo voice)

1   2

♩ ♫ ♩ ♫

gather some ripe fruit

1   2   3

♩ ♫ ♩ ♫ ♩

Chorus
(softly)   ripe fruit, ripe fruit, ripe

Drum and voice percussion	Action
4 ♫ ♩ ♫ fruit, ripe fruit **1 2 3 4** Drum beats ♩ ♫♩ ♫♩ ♫♩ ♫ To (solo voice) **1 2** ♩ ♫ ♩ ♫ bring to his mas-ter **1 2 3 4** Drum ♩ ♫♩ ♫♩ ♫♩ ♫ (Chorus) master, master, master, master,	
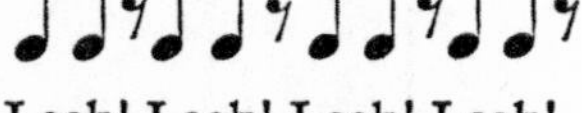 Chorus and drum (urgently)  ♫ ⅞ ♫ ⅞ ♫ ⅞ watch out! watch out! watch out! ♫ ⅞ watch out! ♫⅞♫ ⅞ ♫ ⅞♫⅞ Look! Look! Look! Look!	They attack the servant, shouting, after the voice percussion, "Stone him!" (four times). The servant drags himself along to join the other two.

Drum and voice percussion	Action
 Drum beat	The tenants now band together and plot angrily. They grimly agree that they must take action.
 Solo voice what will they do now?	
 Chorus do now, do now, do now, do now,	
Separate male voice (either from outside narration group or on tape): "What shall I do? I will send my beloved Son; maybe they will respect him."	
Drum beat (urgent) (i)	(i) One tenant directs the others to the four corner points of the vineyard to keep watch.
(ii)	(ii) The tenant directs them to change positions and keep watch again.
(iii)	(iii) All move to DSR to look out for intruders.

Drum and voice percussion	Action
(iv) ♩♩♩ ♩ (triplet with fermata)	(iv) All move to DSL to look out.
♫ 𝄾 ♫ 𝄾 ♫ 𝄾 ♫ 𝄾 ♫ 𝄾 etc.	The tenants creep furtively around the back of the vineyard, still on the look out.
	Jesus now enters behind the vineyard and, to begin with, unnoticed by the tenants, he walks round to the wounded servants and ministers to them.
Drum beat stops at this point.	As the tenants come to the front of the vineyard they see Jesus. The leader calls out in consternation "The Son!" Each in turn echoes his words: "The Son!" "The Son!" "The Son!" etc. The leader calls out "Kill!" and each tenant again takes up the word. They surround Jesus, drag him to the ground and beat him to the words "Kill! Kill! Kill!" (seven times).
Seven drum beats to accentuate the tenants beating Jesus.	
Separate male voice (possibly on tape): "Father, forgive them for they do not know what they are doing".	

The drama could either stop here or could be extended to include a short congregational meditation on Jesus's death. For this, the vineyard, tenants and servants would move out of role and gather round Jesus. Gently they raise him to an upright position as though he were on the cross. For this action, someone kneels down on his own heels with one person standing on either side. Jesus stands on the thighs of the one kneeling, who supports Jesus's legs in front. Each arm of Jesus is held out by one of the standing people. The rest sit on either side as though grieving and mourning.

NARRATOR: "God so loved the world that he gave his only begotten Son that whoever believes in him should not perish but have everlasting life." (John 3:16)

Together, those around the cross sing the first verse of "My song is love unknown". The congregation are then invited to join in singing the other verses, at the end of which Jesus is taken from the cross and carried out, followed by the rest.

The action of this particular piece would not take long though there would possibly be alternative ways of ending. It could lead into a sermon or a series of readings and songs on the theme of Christ's death. It might suitably be used for a Good Friday service or incorporated into a longer anthology of dance drama and music, as in "With Love from Jesus" later in this chapter. It is best to rehearse the voice chorus separately at first and to work towards real clarity and sureness so that the speakers can fit in with those involved in the movement. The lifting of Jesus on to the cross also needs separate and careful practice so that it does not look too awkward but quiet and reverent. The person taking the part of Jesus will need to co-operate in standing on the thighs of his support, but otherwise should let his hands and head flop loosely down.

2. THE LOST SON

Luke 15 contains three stories told by Jesus on the theme of the lost being found—a shepherd finds his sheep which had strayed, a housewife sweeps up her lost coin and a father welcomes home his son who had gone away to a distant country to find independence and freedom. This particular story has much to say to our society today and there are many kinds of lostness to which it speaks. Some have lost a sense of direction in life, some feel acutely a loss of personal identity which may result in loneliness or depression. Some feel a sense of estrangement from God because of their sin and misdoings. These different experiences of lostness may be felt in isolation or in a crowd—a person may look very normal and ordinary on the outside whilst his inner world feels very different. (For this reason, we decided to let one dancer be the son's thoughts and portray something of what was going on in his inner world.) So in this full-length dance drama or anthology, lasting about one hour, we tried to show how the son's decision to stake his claim for independence led him through various experiences to a place of great loneliness and despair from which he eventually returned to his waiting father.

There are four parts to this drama—Introduction, Journey, Far Country and Homecoming—and about sixteen to twenty people are required, including two singers and a narrator. If possible, the dancer taking the part of the son's thoughts should be fairly experienced in mime and dance in order to interpret the two solos well. (A shorter version of this dance drama which does not involve solo dance is incorporated into the anthology "With Love from Jesus", found later in this chapter.)

Introduction

Cast: Father   Drum player
     Elder son   Singer
     Younger son   Narrator
     Voice chorus (four–five)

NARRATOR introduces the story by reading Luke 15:11–14 (*Today's English Version*).

Drum and voice percussion	*Action*
Enter drum player, chorus leader and three or four in the chorus.	Enter father, elder son, younger son. They stand in a triangle with hands on each other's shoulders, indicating unity.

Drum

1   2   3   4

A
(solo voice)

× father
younger
son ×   × elder son

1   2

man had two sons

1   2   3

Chorus

two sons, two sons, two sons

4

two sons.

1   2   3   4   5

two,   two,   two,   two

Drum and voice percussion	Action
Solo the elder	The elder son turns to face audience.
and the younger	The younger son turns to face audience.
1 2 3 4 **Drum**	The younger son begins to pace up and down thoughtfully whilst the father and elder son talk together.
1 2 **Solo** This one's im-por-tant	
1 2 **Chorus** impor-tant, im-portant, im-	
3 4 por-tant, im-por-tant	

Drum and voice percussion	Action
	The younger son pauses to consider them but then continues to pace around, as though formulating a plan.

Drum and voice percussion	*Action*

1   2

♩ ♫ ♩ ♫

want-ing some money

1 2 3 4

♩ ♫♩ ♫♩ ♫♩ ♫

Chorus money, money, money, money

1 2 3 4

He goes to his brother.

Drum ♩ ♫♩ ♫♩ ♫♩ ♫

1   2

♩ ♫ ♩ ♫

Solo First he'll ask his brother·

1 2 3

♩ ♫♩ ♫♩ ♫

Chorus brother, brother, brother,

4 5

♩ ♫ ♩

brother.

Drum and voice percussion	Action
1 2 3 4	"Brother, lend me some money!" His brother refuses and exits. The younger son pauses, wondering what to do next. He looks resentful and peeved.
Drum	
1 2	
Solo Now what's he thinking?	
1 2 3	
Chorus thinking, thinking, thinking,	
4	
thinking.	
1 2 3 4	
Drum	Now the younger son decides to ask his father for his share of the family inheritance.
He's (solo voice)	

Drum and voice percussion	Action
1 **2** going to his fath-er **1** **2** **3** Chorus father, father, father, **4** **5** father.	
1 **2** **3** Chorus owe you, owe you, owe you, **4** **5** owe you.	Son: "Father!"— [in demanding, imperious tones] Father: "My son?" Son: "Give me what you owe me." Father: "What do I owe you?" (Chorus immediately takes up father's words.)

Drum and voice percussion	Action
	Son (as though protesting to audience):"Everything!" (directly to father) "My money!" Father: "My son—" (He sadly gives him his share of money.) Son: "My father—"

Drum and voice percussion	Action
1 2 3 4	
Drum	The younger son abruptly pockets the money and moves away from his father.
He's (solo voice)	
1 2	
going on a journey	His mood begins to change to one of optimism.
1 2 3	
Chorus journey, journey, journey,	
4	
journey.	

Drum and voice percussion	Action
1 **2** **Solo** Where is he going?	
1 **2** **3** **4** **Chorus** going, going, going, going,	He counts the money, considers it with enthusiasm and exits down centre aisle of church. The father moves USL and stands on a small block where he remains throughout the following two scenes.
1 **2** **Solo** Fara-way from home—	
1 **2** **3** **Chorus** fara-way, fara-way, fara-way,	
4 fara-way.	
1 **2** **3** **4** **5** **Drum**	

Song: "Faraway." This may be sung unaccompanied. (See Appendix A (ii) for words and melody.)

Journey

Cast: Father   Eight–ten dancers, including Thought
        Younger son   Drum player

This scene portrays the son's progress to the far country, his anticipation and sense of freedom, but then some of the obstacles and threats involved in such a journey. Always, in the background, is his father.

The son enters from the right walking cheerfully to eight drum beats. Then the group of dancers enter likewise, walking round together, as on a journey and following this sequence (the son included):

eight walking steps, all saying "Go" (eight times);

sixteen slow running steps, all saying "Leaving" (eight times);

eight step-and-jump steps, all saying "Faraway" (eight times). These steps culminate in the dancers leaping up and shouting "I'm free! I'm me!" The son, feeling equally abandoned, also calls out "I'm free! I'm me!" The dancers then start walking around in disorder hurrying and bustling, bumping into the son, preoccupied with their own affairs. The son begins to look confused.

SON: "Help me—I'm a stranger—" (twice).

A dancer pauses briefly to help the son over an obstacle (i.e. another dancer crouching down in his pathway) but hurries on as the son stumbles, too busy to give further help.

SON: "I rely on you—please help me—" He looks round at the others moving around amongst each other, unconcerned about his needs or anyone else's apart from their own. He then meets another obstacle, two dancers barring his way and impeding his progress. So he turns to change direction but trips and falls. The dancers then group either side of the boy's father (who has been standing still on a block silently watching throughout). The father does not relate to his son, for this is only in the son's memory. The dancers now make loving, welcoming arm movements towards the son, quietly singing together in chorus:

Home, come, come, Home, come, come, Home, come, come, Love

(unaccompanied)

The son, remembering his home, reaches out hopefully, as though attracted by the thought of abandoning his journey, but suddenly the dancers, changing mood, turn into a menacing, swirling group, spiralling around the son, leering at him and threatening with angular, spiked movements. As their movements become faster, so they take up some of the words used in this scene, throwing them at the son in a crescendo of sound and taunting him (e.g. "Faraway", "I'm free! I'm me!", "Help me—I'm a stranger", "I rely on you", "Home, home, home"), as though the son's thoughts are sending out several messages at once. He stands cowering in the middle of the swirling group as the speed and volume increase. Then they suddenly rush out, leaving him frightened with his hands over his ears.

As he sinks down to a kneeling position, there rises up behind him a solo dancer, the son's Thought. Whilst he remains kneeling, she portrays in dance and mime some of his mixed thoughts and feelings. Obviously, this needs to be carefully worked out by dancer and producer. We used part of the "Gloriana" Dances by Benjamin Britten (see Appendix A (iii)), and the dancer portrayed through mime and movement: (a) the son's resolution to pursue independence and freedom, and the self-will with which he sets out; (b) his alternating courage and lack of it, as he thinks of the various obstacles on the journey. Then Thought mimes some of the stages of development in the son's relationship with his father; (c) as a child he played with father and walked hand in hand with him; (d) as an adolescent he began to assert himself, sometimes venturing out with bravado, sometimes retreating to father's side; (e) he sees himself as a grown adult, benevolently talking with his friends, drinking and laughing; (f) he imagines himself helping the father along by the arm in old age, and showing him real care; (g) returning to the present, he portrays his ambivalent and violent attitude. What is he to do—go his own way and stake his claim for independence, or return to the safety of his family? How will he measure up to life and the expectations of others? (This indecisiveness can be shown by moving towards the father, then away from him, with the father continuing to watch yet making no movements.) The solo dance ends with Thought deciding to continue his journey to the far country, touching the son on the shoulder, beckoning him to follow. Casting his fears to the winds, the son leaves. Narrator reads poem, "What do I want?" (see

Appendix A (iv)). This poem was written by a student. Ideally one of the group performing might write an original poem on the theme of quest and searching.

Far Country

Cast:

Father (who remains in his former position, still watching, without participating)

Younger son
Dancers, including Thought
Narrator
Singer

With shrieks of laughter and cheers, the dancers rush in from the back, and down the centre aisle. (Use suitable music such as Milhaud's *La Création du Monde*, see Appendix A (v).) They greet each other noisily. A variety of movements and mime can now be improvised portraying gaiety and merry-making—e.g. they are attracted by a procession (unseen) and run to see it, waving and cheering. Then, quickly distracted, they move to another area, teasing each other.

The younger son now enters, seeking popularity and enjoyment. A girl flaunts herself in front of him, to the delight of the group, and the son chases her round the group until he catches her. They cheer and tease him. He then moves off with the girl, and beckons to the rest to come too for a drink, at his expense. This they do with more laughter and back-slapping. One of the men in the group then challenges the son to a game of dice. After two throws —during which the rest are watching attentively, and favouring the son—the other man throws a win. Immediately, the fickle crowd transfer their affections to the winner, surrounding him and leaving the son alone, having gambled away his money. Suddenly they turn on him, pointing accusing fingers and saying, firstly one at a time, then in unison:

"No good!"
"Failure!"
"Wretched!"
"Go!"

The son then repeats the words on his own, hurt and bewildered, and backs away from them. The group then turn their backs on him, slowly lowering their accusing fingers. He is left, on the opposite side to them, slumped in despair.

NARRATOR (to a background of low, howling wind on tape, see Appendix A (vi)): "Then a severe famine spread over that country, and he was left without a thing. So he went to work for one of the citizens of that country, who sent him out to his farm to take care of the pigs. He wished he could fill himself with the bean pods the pigs ate, but no one gave him any."

The group now move across the floor, hungry and groaning as if starving. Someone walks in miming a scattering of bean pods which the group greedily snatch up and they run out. The son, seeing food, moves forward to get some but is too late, the others have taken the little there was.

SON (weak and desolate):
> "I'm lost,
> I'm needy,
> I'm empty,
> I'm falling."

He moves upstage, and falls to his knees in despair and hopelessness.

NARRATOR reads poem "The snapping of the final nerve-string" (or a poem on the theme of loneliness, written by a group member. See Appendix A (vii) for text of this poem.)

SON (moving forward and appealing to the audience for help):
> "Hear me.
> Find me.
> Help me.
> Hold me."

SONG (again on the theme of loneliness or abandonment). We used "Standing Alone" by Judy Mackenzie (see Appendix A (viii)).

At this point, Thought quietly enters and, whilst the son remains still on the ground, performs another solo dance, showing his inner turmoil and anguish. The music we used, portraying in dance some of the song words, was "Inside of me" by Rod McKuen (see Appendix A (ix)).

As the dance finishes, Thought kneels behind the son with one hand on his shoulder, and this position is held while the Narrator reads verses from Psalm 88 (*Living Bible*).

"O God, I have wept before you day and night. Now hear my prayers; oh, listen to my cry, for my life is full of troubles, and death draws near. You have thrust me down to the darkest depths. I am in a trap, with no way out. Why have you thrown my life away? Why are you turning your face from me and looking the other way? Lover, friend, acquaintance—all are gone. There is only darkness everywhere!"

CHORUS (offstage): "Father, home, love, come" (twice).

NARRATOR reads Luke 15:17–20.

Thought gently urges the son to get up and make the journey home. Uncertainly and with faltering steps, the son makes his way down the centre aisle, Thought walking behind him with one hand still on his shoulder, as though directing him.

Homecoming

Cast: Father   Chorus of eight–twelve
       Son   Two singers

The chorus enter, divide into two groups and stand at either side of the front area, facing the audience. Alternately, they recite verses from Psalm 25 (*Living Bible*).

Group A recite verses 4–7.
Group B recite verses 8–10.
Group A recite verse 11.
Group B recite verses 12–13a.
Group A recite verses 15–16a.

Both groups, in unison, extending their arms in a gesture of loving welcome:
"Come, Lord, mercy,
Come, Lord, mercy,
Come, come, come, come."

SONG: "Come to the Father" (see Appendix A (x)). An alternative could be "Come unto Him", from Handel's *Messiah*. As the song begins, the father steps down from his watching position at the back, and stands upstage, looking for his son's return. The son walks slowly and painfully up the centre aisle from the back of the church. As he comes to the front, he stumbles and his father comes forward to help him. The father gently leads him upstage between the two groups of chorus, who look on, welcoming and compassionate. As the song ends, there is a final piece of dialogue between father and son.

FATHER: "Son!"
SON: "Father."
FATHER: "Give me what you owe me."
SON (fearfully): "What do I owe you?" (The chorus softly take up his words, "owe you", four times.)
SON: "What *do* I owe you?"
FATHER (pause): "Nothing!"
SON: "My father!"
FATHER: "My son!" (warmly and tenderly they embrace).

3. KOINŌNIA (a New Testament Greek word meaning 'Fellowship')

This visual meditation in movement is meant to portray the togetherness, sharing and love which should characterise Christ's followers and the cost of such fellowship. It incorporates several pieces of teaching from the New Testament describing the quality of sharing found amongst the early Christians. Paul describes the interrelatedness of the Christian Church as "the Body of Christ" and teaches that it is this kind of close unity and integration which we are called to demonstrate to the world. In this drama we first see division instead of unity, bondage instead of freedom, suspicion and exclusive attitudes. These sins are amongst those to which Christ comes with his ministry of deliverance. But by many he is not welcomed for they prefer their divisions and differences. They reject his love, fall to fighting one another and then, turning their attentions on him, they attack and kill him, nailing him to a cross. Seeing what they have done, some repent and come to the foot of the cross for forgiveness whilst others walk away from the scene of their crime. There is also a suggested alternative ending which allows for the drama to extend into a congregational response.

Cast: Jesus   Narrator
     Three groups of four or more people   Percussion player
     (preferably more)

On one empty wall there is a large cross. This could either be of wood, leaning against the wall, or of paper fixed to the wall.

Action

Music: fade up Lento movement from Vaughan Williams' "London" Symphony. After a few moments fade down while NARRATOR reads:

NARRATOR: "A new commandment I give to you, that you love one another; even as I have loved you, that you also love one another. By this all men will know that you are my disciples, if you have love for one another." (John 13:34, 35)

Enter three groups of people, A, B and C. They remain in their separate groups, all taking up positions of bondage and sorrow.

Group A sit cross-legged with wrists apparently bound like prisoners.

Ground B stand with wrists bound.

Group C kneel up, also with wrists bound.

GROUP A: In turn, each person says a phrase from 1 Corinthians 12:25, 26, where Paul describes liberty and sharing—yet their bodily attitudes deny this. "No discord", "care for one another", "all weep together", "all rejoice together".

Then in unison Group A say "We are the body of Christ". They lean forward extending their bound wrists in sorrow.

NARRATOR: "This is my commandment, that you love one another as I have loved you." (John 15:12)

GROUP B: In turn each person says a phrase from Acts 2:44ff. which describes the joyful community and sharing of the early Christians. But again their attitudes of bondage and sorrow deny the reality of the words they speak. "All things in common", "together", "glad and generous hearts", "praising God".

Unison: "We are the body of Christ". They lean forward, showing their bound wrists and groaning.

NARRATOR: "This is my commandment, that you love one another as I have loved you."

GROUP C: Each person says a phrase from James 5:16 where the writer speaks of the need for loving mutuality and concern. But the members of this group are not concerned for each other and again their attitudes deny what they say. "Confess your sins to one another", "pray for one another", "be healed".

Unison: "We are the body of Christ." Again they extend bound wrists to indicate they cannot meet each other's needs.
(Music off.)

NARRATOR: "Where there is no vision the people perish."
In their separate groups and swaying sadly, they all say
          "Perish, perish, perish, perish":

DRUM BEATS: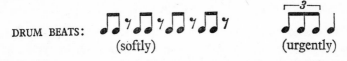
          (softly)   (urgently)

At the urgent note of the drum, the three groups leap back in alarm to face each other in fear and suspicion, their wrists no longer bound. One person from Group B moves cautiously and pleadingly to Group C for acceptance but is rejected. Two from Group A move towards Group B but are also rejected. Each group continues its attitude of hostility.

At this point each group could work out some activity which emphasises their exclusiveness and preoccupation. Suggest that they work this out on their own as a piece of group work which can then be discussed and evaluated by everyone. This will provide an opportunity for group initiative and self-direction. The producer could offer a few ideas which could be used or not (e.g. pre-occupation with 'the daily round, the common task' or with solitary activities, materialistic concern, self-engrossment). In one group who were performing this drama each person drew an imaginary circle around himself on the floor, sat in it and began to mime some activity like eating, sleeping, reading, filing her nails, looking into a mirror, with complete disregard for the others. At a drum beat they all yawned, lay down and slept, then, at another signal, awoke and resumed the same activity, still with no aware-

ness that there were others close by them. It described well how
we often cut off from each other in daily life. Each group should be
clear about what they are trying to portray, which should be kept
simple and short, unhurried and clear. It is probably best to use
mime throughout rather than introduce words in order to
emphasise the loneliness of people who are together yet separated.

NARRATOR: "A new commandment I give to you, that you love
one another; even as I have loved you, that you also love one
another. By this all men will know that you are my disciples, if
you have love for one another."

MUSIC: Fade up second movement of Violin Concerto, op. 14
(1939) by Samuel Barber (see Appendix A (xi)). Jesus enters and
stands for a moment looking from one group to another in sorrow.

JESUS: "This is my commandment, that you love one another
as I have loved you." (John 15:12)

With compassion he moves towards each group in turn who all
shrink away from him. He indicates to them that he would have
them together, united and caring, but they cannot respond to this.
He then stretches up to heaven, as though beseeching his Father.
The three groups watch him curiously. Jesus then looks at the
large cross on the wall. At first he shrinks from it, then he goes up
to it and touches it. He walks away from it and kneels with his
face in his hands. He then slowly stretches out each arm and looks
at the palms of his hands.

JESUS: "Greater love has no man than this, that a man lays down
his life for his friends." (John 15:13)
Then he kneels silently facing the cross, in prayer.

NARRATOR: "I am praying for them; I am not praying for the
world but for those whom thou hast given me, for they are thine;
all mine are thine, and thine are mine, and I am glorified in them.
And now I am no more in the world, but they are in the world,
and I am coming to thee. Holy Father, keep them in thy name,
which thou hast given me, that they may be one, even as we are
one.
"I made known unto them thy name, and I will make it known,
that the love with which thou hast loved me may be in them, and
I in them." (John 17:9-11, 26)

An individual from each of the three groups tentatively approaches Jesus in fear, curiosity, amazement. But they quickly return to their groups calling out:

GROUP A: "Leave us alone!" (each person in the group echoes the word "alone—alone—alone—alone".)

GROUP B: "It's safer apart!" (each echoes the word "apart—apart—apart—apart".)

GROUP C: "We'd rather be separate!" (each echoes the word "separate—separate—separate—separate".)

Dance of anger and hostility

The idea of this section is that the slow, sorrowful mood which has predominated so far now becomes stronger and more vicious. Individuals attack those from other groups and all become vindictive, culminating in an angry attack on Jesus himself. The producer could work out with the groups a succession of movements depicting attack and fighting. Some very effective music for this might be *The Tempest* by Honegger (see Appendix A (xii)). Dramatic fighting needs considerable body control and careful rehearsing. It is best for a couple fighting to plot out together each movement in a matching balance of offensive and defensive actions. Avoid fussy movements and try to make the mime very clear and visually effective, using very stylised, slow motion actions.

An alternative scripted sequence of movements:

(a)   a person from A rushes towards one in C to fight;
      a person from B rushes towards one in A to fight;
      a person from C rushes towards one in B to fight (see Figure i, p. 167).

(b)   Others in each group form pairs, back to back either kneeling or standing, lifting their bound wrists and chanting, to the beat of the drum (two drum beats to a word):
      A—alone, alone, alone alone (followed by)
      B—apart, apart, apart, apart (followed by)
      C—separate, separate, separate, separate.

(c)   The three individuals now rejoin their own groups, leading them round in three separate circles in stamping steps, accompanied by the drum and each saying the same word as before, eight times each. As they stamp round their heads are thrown back and their bound hands thrust into the air in front of them (see Figure ii, opposite).

(d)   In each group, individuals now turn against each other. The drum continues its regular beat.

(e)   Group A rush against group C to overcome them. C retaliate, driving them back. B now rush against C and, again, C drive them back.

(f)   Jesus pleads in turn with each group but they angrily brush him aside.

(g)   Someone from Group A suddenly points vindictively at Jesus and, treating him as their scapegoat, all start circling round him, pointing accusing fingers at him. He is now the focus of their attention. They circle round him like animals waiting to pounce on a victim, gradually closing in and raising their fists in fury (see Figure iii, opposite).

The drum keeps up a steady beat and, if more cumulative volume is needed, the dancers could chant their group words as they stamp round (i.e. "alone", "apart", "separate").

(h)   At a sharp signal from the drum the circling and chanting cease and the dancers remain motionless and silent for a brief moment, one arm raised as though to attack. They are, by now, in a tight group around Jesus.

(i)   JESUS: "Love one another."

(j)   Shrieking in protest, all beat Jesus to the ground, then stand silently looking down at him.

NARRATOR: "Greater love has no man than this, that a man lay down his life for his friends."

Jesus is now nailed to the cross. He could be carried to the wall where the cross is and propped against it. He should let his head droop down on to his chest, as though dead.

Seeing the consequences of their actions, the group members adopt different attitudes and different postures. Some stand or sit awe-struck. Others mourn and weep. Some turn away in distaste. (It is important in working out the positions really to discuss

Fig i

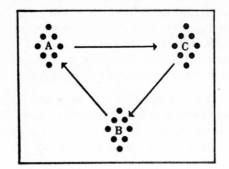

Fig ii

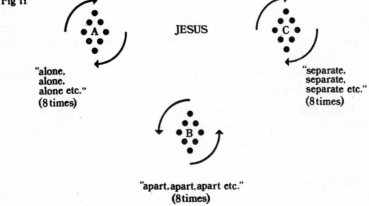

JESUS

"alone,
alone,
alone etc."
(8 times)

"separate,
separate,
separate etc."
(8 times)

"apart, apart, apart etc."
(8 times)

Fig iii

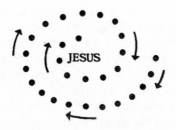

JESUS

people's personal reactions both to what they have done and to Jesus on the cross. Different individuals will probably have very differing reactions and the positions they adopt should reflect with integrity their own thinking and feeling.) In grouping around the cross, use a variety of levels—standing, kneeling, sitting, lying— with some people alone and others joining together.

NARRATOR: "In this is love, not that we loved God but that he loved us and sent his Son to be the expiation for our sins. Beloved, if God so loved us, we also ought to love one another. We love, because he first loved us." (1 John 4:10, 11, 19)

The drama could stop at this point, with four people carrying Jesus out and the others slowly processing out behind him. In this case the emphasis would be on the price paid by Christ to gain fellowship for us. This point might then be taken up in a short talk addressed to the congregation, emphasising that Christ, by his death, broke the power of our hostilities, animosities and separations so that we might experience a true fellowship and sharing that centre upon him.

An alternative ending might be this one, following straight on from the previous ending.

NARRATOR: "If we say we have no sin, we deceive ourselves, and the truth is not in us. If we confess our sins, he is faithful and just, and will forgive our sins and cleanse us from all unrighteousness." (1 John 1:8, 9)

Each person comes up to the cross with a private confession of sin. This is not, of course, 'acting', but something deeply real and thoughtfully prepared. It will previously have been suggested that people consider something particular which they want to bring to Christ for forgiveness. In explaining this, remember the theme of the drama. "In what ways have I sinned against others—in the church fellowship? In the youth group? In this dance-drama group? Have I fought for recognition? Have I been unco-operative? Have I withheld myself from others who needed me? Have I shown partiality? Impatience? Have I not made efforts in sharing with my own family?" etc. This is not an invitation to lengthy introspection but rather to own up to unacceptable and wrong attitudes and to bring them to Christ for forgiveness.

This act of people coming to Jesus could be done against some suitable music (e.g. Chorale, "Commit thy ways to Jesus" from Bach's *St. Matthew Passion*). After all have come, they could join together informally into twos and threes (including the person taking the part of Jesus) and share in conversation or prayer. Obviously this would be more suitable if there were no audience, though if it took place in church and the congregation were prepared beforehand, everyone could be invited to turn to each other for informal sharing and prayer or could be invited to go and spend a few minutes with someone less known to them in the church. In this way the whole point of 'Koinōnia' would be realised and the theme would have moved from its dramatic structure into the real-life situation. A complete experimental service could be worked out on this theme with many opportunities for learning together more of the reality of fellowship.

After taking part in this particular dance drama, one young man wrote to me of what he had learnt through it: ". . . it enabled me to appreciate for the first time on an emotional level the meaning of Christ's death on the cross. Up till now I have known and appreciated the fact on an intellectual basis but not emotionally. So for me this is a real step forward and something I have been praying about for some time."

4. With Love from Jesus

Occasionally a whole service—perhaps a guest service—might be devoted to a dance-drama presentation. Having worked out several such scripts in our own group, through which we learnt some important lessons, we decided to attempt a portrayal of Christ's ministry, using movement, mime, words and music. We wanted some, if not all, of the music to be written by group members so that together we could work at some of the communication difficulties involved. Our primary aim was to teach, sharing through these media a true and artistically valid picture of Christ's ministry. But we also wanted to stimulate worship of Christ. We involved about thirty people in movement, music-making, reading and percussion effects and the production lasted about an hour. We incorporated some of the material we had used before but really tried to integrate it carefully into a new unity. The drama was in three consecutive parts:

Part I—Preparation for ministry:
    Jesus's baptism
    Temptation
    Jesus calls his disciples
Part II—Jesus's ministry:
    The ten lepers
    The adulterous woman
    The lost son
Part III—The way of the Cross and after:
    The parable of the vineyard
    Death and resurrection
    Pentecost, the commission, the promise of Christ's return

Since we knew we would be performing in a variety of church buildings we made the staging as simple as possible. Once or twice we used straightforward spotlights, though were not dependent on these.

Part I: Preparation for ministry

Cast: Jesus   Twelve disciples
       Three groups of temptations,
          four in each group

1. *Jesus's baptism*

Already in position—though as inconspicuous as possible—are three groups of temptations, with four or five people in each. To start with they crouch to the ground in stillness, heaped together in groups as if three large rocks.

Jesus walks up the centre aisle to the front, turns and kneels. (Male voice on tape): "This is my beloved son in whom I am well pleased."

Jesus rises in an attitude of response and thanksgiving to his Father. Immediately after this commissioning, his calling is tested.

2. *Temptation*

(Taped sound effect of wailing wind. For extra effect and volume, alternate wind with phrases of electronic music. See Appendix A (xiii) for details.)

In alarm Jesus looks round and sees the three sinister groups of temptations leering at him with threatening gestures. First Group A come to life, moving towards Jesus, pointing and accusing. (Fade down wind.)

GROUP A (unison): "If . . . if . . . if . . . if . . .
                  If you are the Son of God"
(each in turn)   "If . . . if . . . if . . . if . . ."
(each person then suggests a line of action that the Son of God might take)

                  e.g. "Feed yourself!"
                       "Keep your strength up!"
                       "Exercise your power!"
                       "Turn these stones into bread!"
(unison, loudly)   "*If* you are the Son of God"
(each in turn, softly) "If . . . if . . . if . . . if . . ."

As each speaks, he points a finger or elbow or fist aggressively or derisively. Each one in the group should adopt a different position and use different levels. Jesus reels back from their accusations, disturbed.

JESUS: "It is written, 'Man shall not live by bread alone, but by every word that proceeds from the mouth of God'."

(Fade up wind) As Group A withdraw into silence and crouch down again, Group B are already beginning to move towards Jesus. They whirl around him, buffeting and mocking him, then resume their group position. (Fade down wind.)

GROUP B (unison): "If . . . if . . . if . . . if . . .
                  If you are the Son of God."
(each in turn)   "If . . . if . . . if . . . if . . ."
(Each again mockingly suggests a way in which Jesus could escape from his quandary.)

                  "Come out of obscurity!"
                  "Perform a stunt!"
                  "Show them you're the greatest!"

"Take the upper hand!"
(unison)   "*If* you are the Son of God."
(each in turn) "If . . . if . . . if . . . if . . ."

Again, Jesus backs away in horror from their suggestions and attack refusing to go the way of fulfilling popular expectations.

JESUS: "It is written, 'You shall not tempt almighty God'."

(Fade up wind.) As Group B withdraw, Group C begin their menacing. One of them approaches Jesus to wrestle with him. He brings him to the ground then returns to the group. Jesus is panting on his knees. (Fade down wind.)

GROUP C (unison): "If . . . if . . . if . . . if . . .
                        If you *are* the Son of God."
(Each suggests to Jesus a way of escape. This group's tactic is subtle compromise.)
                        "I'll give you power—"
                        "—and riches"
                        "—and success"
(unison)   "If you *are* the Son of God."
(each in turn)   "If . . . if . . . if . . . if . . ."

JESUS (with authority): "Satan, get away! It is written, 'You shall worship the Lord your God and serve him alone'." (Fade up wind.)

The three groups of temptations whirl around Jesus in spiralling movements, threatening, yet not daring to get too close to him. They exit. (Wind and music off.)

Jesus kneels in prayer.

3. *Jesus calls his disciples*

Jesus now rises to walk away, but Andrew runs to meet him from a point nearby.

ANDREW: "Sir—"

JESUS: "Andrew—"

ANDREW (running across to Simon Peter who is standing some way off): "Come and see—it's the Messiah!"
(They go to Jesus, Simon Peter hesitantly.)

JESUS: "You are Simon, John's son, but you shall be called Peter, the Rock. Come, follow me."

The other disciples, James, John, Philip, Bartholomew, Thomas, Matthew, James, Simon, Thaddaeus, Judas, are waiting at different points in the church. One by one Jesus calls them by name. They come to him and begin quietly talking amongst themselves. Once he has gathered his disciples, they sing together:

> "Follow, follow, follow Jesus,
> Follow Jesus where he leads."

(For rest of words and melody, see Appendix A (xiv).)

This simple song can be sung as a round whilst the group walks together round the church and back up the central aisle.

When back at the front again, the disciples sit around Jesus who stands in their midst.

JESUS: "The Spirit of the Lord is upon me.
He has anointed me to preach the Good News to the poor,
He has sent me to proclaim liberty to the captives,
And recovery of sight to the blind,
To set free the oppressed,
To announce the year when the Lord will save his people!"

Together Jesus and his disciples exit.

At the end of Part I a suitable solo or duet could be sung, such as "Consider Him" (see Appendix A (xv)).

Part II: Jesus's ministry

In this section we see some of the ways in which Jesus fulfilled his commission to teach, heal and deliver. The kind of person he was is clear as we witness some of the personal encounters he had with those who came to him for healing, forgiveness and to find their identity.

1. The ten lepers

Cast: Jesus   One drummer
      Ten Lepers   Narrator

First come the lepers, twisted and deformed, regarded as outcasts by society and without hope of recovery. To these untouchables (and we still have many different kinds of 'lepers' in our society today) he brings healing and wholeness. Their joy is great but only one returns to give thanks.

Introduction: NARRATOR reads the story from Luke 17:11-19. The action follows the pattern set out in full in chapter 4, so it will not be duplicated here.

At the end, after the thankful leper has returned, there is a pause for reflection before continuing with the next piece.

2. *The adulterous woman*

Cast: Jesus   Seven-eight Pharisees
       Woman   Singer
       Four-five disciples   Narrator

Next we see Jesus's great understanding and compassion as he is confronted by a woman whose sin has been heartlessly exposed by the Pharisees, the legalists of Jesus's day. Not only does he save her from physical death but, by his non-judgmental attitude, his forgiveness and acceptance of her save her from her own degradation and shame.

Introduction: NARRATOR reads part of the story from John 8:3-5.

A group of five-six Pharisees enter and stand in a group to one side, talking together. They look self-righteous and hard. Jesus enters from the opposite side with some of his disciples, discussing with them. Suddenly there is a noisy disturbance and three Pharisees enter hounding and dragging along a poor woman, threatening and cursing her. If possible they should enter through the congregation down the centre aisle, using such phrases as:

"Disgusting!"
"Filthy cur!"
"You'll pay for this—"
"It'll be a stoning for you, young woman!" etc.

They fling her down on the ground in front of Jesus whilst the rest look on with distaste and curiosity.

PHARISEE 1: "Teacher, here's an adulteress. The law of Moses commands us to stone her to death. What do you say?"

(Pharisees take up attitude of hostility.) Jesus silently bends down and writes on the ground with his finger. They watch with curiosity.

PHARISEE 2: "Well, teacher, what's *your* opinion?"

JESUS (standing and facing the accusers): "Let him who is sinless throw the first stone at her." (He then bends down to write again on the ground.) Several Pharisees quickly pick up stones and make as though to hurl them at the woman. But as they see Jesus's face they drop the stones and resentfully back away. They remain in a hostile group at some distance from the woman and Jesus, but still watching. Gradually the woman starts to pull herself up to a sitting position. At first she is too fearful to look at Jesus, expecting judgment from him, and keeps her eyes averted.

SONG: "I cannot meet his pure, pure gaze."

(For words and music see Appendix A (xvi). This is best sung as a solo with organ or piano accompaniment.)

Eventually the woman is able to look into Jesus's face and see his acceptance of her.

JESUS: "Woman, where are your accusers? Has no one condemned you?"

WOMAN: "No one, Lord."

JESUS: "Neither do I. Go, and do not sin again."

PHARISEE I (with a sneer): "He even forgives sinners!"

Gradually the woman is able to accept that she has been forgiven. With great joy and love she dances out, in a short solo dance, her penitence and thanksgiving to Jesus whilst the disciples look on. She finishes by kneeling in adoration at Jesus's feet. He beckons the disciples to come near and places one of the woman's hands into one of the disciple's. The group remain around Jesus for a quiet moment. In sad contrast, the Pharisees resentfully walk out, angry at what has happened.

3. *The lost son*

Cast: Father	Narrator
Elder son	Drum player
Younger son	Voice chorus (three–four, who can
Ten dancers	be from amongst the dancers)

The theme of loving acceptance is continued in the parable of the prodigal son who journeys into a far country, squandering his money, health and reputation. But finally, coming to his senses, he returns to his father who has steadfastly continued to love him and whose thoughts have followed him throughout. The welcome home is unconditional, without recrimination or scoldings. The son who was lost has been found. (The following action is a shortened version of the full script found earlier in this chapter.)

(a) *Introduction:* NARRATOR reads part of the story from Luke 15:11-13. The main characters are then introduced through mime and voice percussion (see p. 148).

(b) *The Far Country.* To loud music (e.g. *La Création du Monde* by Milhaud, see Appendix A (v)) and with cheering and laughter, ten dancers rush down the centre aisle, greeting each other, waving and cheering. They move around in excited groups miming actions, as though at a fair or festival. The younger son enters, looking for popularity and fun. He chases a girl, catches her and is cheered by the crowd. After a round of drinks, one of the men challenges the younger son to a game of dice. After a few throws, the son loses his money and his popularity and the crowd turn on him, pointing accusing fingers and saying, in chorus:
"no good, failure, wretched, go!" (three times)

NARRATOR: reads Luke 15:14b-16. (As a background, play taped wind effects.) The group now act out their hunger, groaning and searching over the ground for scraps of food. They then exit and the son is left desolate on the ground.

SON (appealing to audience): "Hear me, find me, help me, hold me!"

NARRATOR reads verses from Psalm 88 (*Living Bible*) which emphasise the son's misery and degradation.
"O God, I have wept before you day and night. Now hear my prayers; oh, listen to my cry, for my life is full of troubles, and death draws near. You have thrust me down to the darkest depths. I am in a trap with no way out. Why have you thrown my life away? Why are you turning your face from me and looking the other way? Lover, friend, acquaintance—all are gone. There is only darkness everywhere."

CHORUS (offstage): "Father, home, love, come." (twice)
Uncertainly the son rises and slowly walks out.

NARRATOR: reads Luke 15:17–20.

(c) *The homecoming*
The father now moves from the place where he has stood during the previous scene and stands centre back. Each side of him is a group of about five or six (the original disciples) sitting or kneeling in attitudes of welcome. Together they say: "Father, home, love, come" whilst the son, slowly and in shame, starts walking from the back, down the centre aisle, towards his father. As he walks, a song is sung, either as a duet or by the two welcoming groups.

SONG: "Come to the Father."
(Words and music in Appendix A (x).)
The son stumbles as he approaches his father, who comes forward to help him complete his homeward journey. As the song ends, there is a short dialogue between father and son (see p. 161).

After a brief pause, Jesus gathers his disciples around him and continues to teach them about the true meaning of love.

JESUS: "This is how God showed his love for us: he sent his only son into the world that we might have life through him. This is what love is: it is not that we have loved God, but that he loved us and sent his son to be the means by which our sins are forgiven." (1 John 4:9, 10)
Together the disciples sing: "Jesus, I love you" (no. 31, *Songs of Fellowship*, Fountain Trust).
Exeunt.

Part III: The way of the cross and after

1. The parable of the vineyard

The Father's love and patience are seen again in the parable of the vineyard where the servants are sent to collect their master's dues. Each is beaten up. Finally the owner sends his son, but he too is rejected, killed and placed in a tomb. (For detailed instructions, see earlier in this chapter, p 135.)

2. Death and resurrection

As the Son is lifted on to the cross, those who formed the vine-yard gather around the foot of the cross as onlookers, remaining there, during the singing of a congregational hymn.

Congregational hymn: "O my Saviour lifted."

During the hymn, Jesus is lowered from the cross into a tomb. He is lifted down carefully, placed on the floor and surrounded by a small circle of people, kneeling with their arms stretched out to cover and enclose Jesus.

At the end of the hymn, to a cymbal clash, those forming the tomb move quickly up, flinging their arms up, and, from their midst, Jesus stands, risen from death. He remains standing whilst the small group move out to join the larger circle, all kneeling. One by one, each person in the circle turns to the next to proclaim Christ's resurrection.

e.g. Person 1: "The Lord is risen!"

Person 2: "He's risen indeed!"

Person 3: "The Lord is risen!"

Person 4: "He's risen indeed!" etc., until the good news has been passed around the whole group, then, together, they all say "Hallelujah!" stretching out towards Jesus.

Jesus now moves to different individuals in the circle to offer his personal resurrection appearance.

THOMAS: "Unless I see the nail prints for myself, *I* shan't believe."

JESUS: "Put your hands here, Thomas. [Indicating his hands and side.] Stop your doubting and believe."

THOMAS: "My Lord and my God!"

JESUS: "Blessed are you, Thomas, because you have believed. But how much more blessed are those who have not seen yet believe."

Mary is bowed with grief and weeping and does not recognise Jesus.

JESUS: "Why are you crying?"

MARY: "If you're the gardener and have taken away his body, tell me where you have put him so that I can go and find him."

JESUS: "Mary—"

MARY (recognising Jesus speaking her name): "Master!"

JESUS: "Do not cling to me because I have not yet returned to my Father. But go to my brothers and tell them from me that I go back to him who is my Father and your Father, my God and your God."

JESUS: "Simon Peter, do you love me more than these?"
PETER: "Yes, Lord, you know that I love you."
JESUS: "Take care of my lambs.—Simon Peter, do you love me?"
PETER: "Yes, Lord, you know that I love you."
JESUS: "Take care of my sheep.—Simon Peter, do you love me?"
PETER: "Lord, you know everything: you know that I love you!"
JESUS: "Take care of my sheep."

JESUS (facing congregation): "On this faith I shall build my church and the gates of hell shall not prevail against it. I will send upon you what my Father has promised. But you must wait in the city until the power from above comes down upon you."
Exeunt.

3. *Pentecost*

As in the upper room in Jerusalem, the disciples kneel in a circle, holding hands and making slow, irregular arm movements, reaching upwards as if in prayers of praise and adoration, and outwards as if in intercession for the world. (This can effectively be done to the background music of "Cast thy burden upon the Lord" from *Elijah* by Mendelssohn.)

Upon this praying group comes the Holy Spirit in a joyful dance of Pentecost. First there comes whirling in a group representing the wind (it can look very effective if chiffon scarves are tied around wrists, in colours ranging through white, grey and blue). They whirl around the startled disciples (use a background of wind sound effect) in spiralling movements. Then another group dances in, representing fire (with scarves ranging through yellow, orange, red, brown, purple). They dance in and out of the bewildered disciples. Gradually fade the wind effect into some suitable music of rejoicing (e.g. part of "Thanks be to God" from *Elijah*) and work out a joyful dance in which all take part, to demonstrate that the Spirit of the risen Christ has now come upon his followers.

At the end of the dance, the dancers pause in positions of praise and joy. Then they hear Christ's commission to them (preferably on tape): "Go to all peoples everywhere and make them my disciples: baptise them in the name of the Father and of the Son and of the Holy Spirit, and teach them to obey everything I have commanded you. And remember, I will be with you always, to the end of the age."

They all now joyfully move out from the front of the church down the different aisles towards the back, singing "Come and bless, Come and praise" (no. 1, *Songs of Fellowship*, Fountain Trust). As they reach the back of the church they pause to hear the declaration of Christ's return (preferably on tape): "This Jesus, who was taken up from you into heaven, will come back in the same way that you saw him go to heaven." All the dancers now return to the front of the church, using different entrance points, walking slowly and reverently, singing "Alleluia" (*Sound of Living Waters*, Hodder and Stoughton). When they reach the front they take up different positions of praise and adoration, facing the altar.

As a final act of worship, and remaining in their positions, they sing:

> "O Come, let us adore him (three times)
> Christ the Lord.
> For he alone is worthy (three times)
> Christ the Lord.
> We'll give him all the glory (three times)
> Christ the Lord."

Since the tune is well known, the congregation could join in also, after which there could be a few moments of silence for reflection and prayer.

This particular anthology lasts about an hour. We used it several times for special guest services in churches and it proved to be very effective. It really did seem to have teaching value. Both young and older people became deeply involved as they watched and, at the end, many stood up, coming into the aisles and to the front of the church as their own response of adoration. On two occasions there was a reaction of deep silence during which people knelt in prayer.

Notes

Chapter 1

1 Francis A. Schaeffer, *Art and the Bible* (Hodder and Stoughton).
2 W. O. E. Oesterley, *The Sacred Dance: A Study in Comparative Folklore* (C.U.P.).
3 J. H. Eaton, "Dancing in the Old Testament", *Worship and Dance* (University of Birmingham Institute for the Study of Worship and Religious Architecture).
4 J. G. Davies, "Towards a Theology of the Dance", *Worship and Dance* (University of Birmingham Institute for the Study of Worship and Religious Architecture).

Chapter 2

1 Andy Kelso, *Drama in Worship* (Grove Books), p. 11.
2 Jane Winearls, "Dance in Church: a personal note", *Worship and Dance*, p. 32 (University of Birmingham Institute for the Study of Worship and Religious Architecture), ed. Prof. J. G. Davies.
3 Andy Kelso, op. cit., p. 12.

Chapter 3

1 Violet R. Bruce and Joan D. Tooke, *Lord of the Dance* (Pergamon Press), p. 7.

Chapter 5

1 Derek Kidner, *Commentary on Psalms* (Tyndale Old Testament Commentaries, I.V.P.), Vol. II, p. 383.

Chapter 7

1 André Louf, *Teach Us To Pray* (Darton, Longman and Todd), p. 60.
2 W. J. Hollenweger, "The Social and Ecumenical Significance of Pentecostal Liturgy", *Studia Liturgica*, 8/4, 1971–2, pp. 207–15. Also "Danced Documentaries—The Theological and Political Significance of Pentecostal Dancing", *Worship and Dance*, p. 81 (University of Birmingham Institute for the Study of Worship and Religious Architecture), ed. Prof. J. G. Davies.

Appendix A: Source Material

(i)   *Lord, Have Mercy*

1. Lord, have mercy, mercy, mercy,
   Lord, have mercy,
   Listen to my prayer.

2. Lord, I was crying,
   Heart inside me dying,
   Lord, may I ask you
   Why weren't you there?

3. Time passes by me,
   Soul of sorrow hides me,
   Lord, in your mercy
   Why weren't you there?

4. Lord, have mercy, mercy, mercy,
   Lord if you made me,
   Why don't you care?

Words and music by Anne Henderson

183

(ii)   *Faraway*

1. Away, faraway,
   Faraway from home,
   Is it life that you are seeking?
   Faraway from home.

2. Hopes, dreams, ambitions,
   Kaleidoscope, round your mind,
   Is this the path that draws you?
   Faraway from home?

3. The way is getting steep now,
   The light is growing dim,
   Where will your journey take you?
   Faraway from home.

4. La, la (Continue to "la" to melody,
   gradually fading away at end.)

Words and music by Rosalind Patterson

A minor *Slowly and wistfully*

(iii) The Courtly Dances from "Gloriana", by Benjamin Britten,
March and Courante (RCA Victor, SB 6635 LSC 2730).

(iv)   *What Do I Want?*

What do I want and where do I go in life?
What purpose and what aims?
And what mirage
through the haze of the heat
of the hot bodies standing?
Now and the future twisted

are one strand,
slender and breakable,
cut it through with a knife—
or hang myself with it—
perhaps—
or, straining against an
unseeable, glass
(though harsh) restraint
of my own formed standards.
But will it break
or shatter from the strain
and the stress of the leaning?
Or, the light too strong
and the notes too strident,
crack and crumble
to dust and dust?
My dust, my form,
my image.
Once more I turn again
and where am I
where am I
going?

Beryl Bates

(v) *La Création du Monde* by Milhaud (HMV, ASD 2316).
(This record is not banded into movements. The excerpt suggested is the second major section and theme, occurring approximately one-third through the track.)

(vi) BBC Sound Effects, record No. 3 (BBC Records, Red 102 M).
(There are eight Sound Effects records in this series, covering a very wide range of useful effects.)

(vii)   *The Snapping of the Final Nerve-String*

The snapping of the final nerve-string
Flings me back into a wilderland
      I have created for myself.
Self is the secret of the silent snake,
The following footfalls or the searing scream,
And I surprise myself—I had not known
The fearfulness of being alone.

The others cannot touch me, cannot touch,
Their terror traps them into tiny spaces,
The places of discovery
That self is nothing more
    Than a terror-trap.

Ann Dunt

(viii) Song "Standing Alone" from album *Judy* by Judy Mackenzie
(Bradbury Wood Ltd.).

(ix) Song "Inside of Me" from *Rod McKuen Live in London* (Warner
Brothers, K66005. WSD 3007).

(x)   *Come to the Father*

1. Come to the Father,
    See, he is waiting,
    Waiting and loving,
    Loving you home.

2. He knows your sorrow,
    He knows your hunger.
    He knows your fearfulness,
    Loving you home.

3. Humble your feelings,
    Welcome forgiveness,
    Hasten your footsteps,
    He's loving you home.

4. Love seeks no payment,
    Come empty-handed,
    See what he offers,
    Loving you home.

Words and music by Anne Long

Not too quickly

Come to the Fa - ther, see he is wait - ing,

G   D   G   D   D   G   D7   G

Wait - ing and lov - ing, Lov - ing you home.

G   G7   C   Am7   G   D7   G

(xi) Second movement (Andante). Concerto for violin and orchestra, opus 14 (1939) by Samuel Barber (World Record Club, RMC CM 59).

(xii) *Prélude pour "La Tempête"* by Honegger (World Record Club, RMC CM 61).

(xiii) Wind sound effect (see previous section (vi)).

(xiv)   *Follow, Follow*

1.   Follow, follow,
     Follow Jesus,
     Follow Jesus
     Where he leads.

2.   He will guide us,
     He will guide us,
     He will guide us
     All the way.

3. He will strengthen,
   He will strengthen,
   He will strengthen,
   Every day.

4. Follow, follow,
   Follow Jesus,
   Follow Jesus
   Where he leads.

Words and music by Anne Long

G minor *(not too quickly)*

Fol-low, fol-low, Fol-low Je-sus. . Fol-low Je - sus where he leads.

(xv) Song "Consider Him" from album "Sounds of Fresh Waters" by Merla Watson (Gordon V. Thompson Ltd., Toronto).

(xvi)   *I Cannot Meet His Pure, Pure Gaze*

1. I cannot meet his pure, pure gaze
   It sees right through my guise,
   Unveils the wrong, exposes sham
   And spotlights all the lies.
   I cannot meet his pure, pure gaze
   Those searching, love-filled eyes.

2. I cannot look into his eyes
   As with the other men,
   Yet they undress me with their gaze
   Degrade me once again,
   It is his innocence that hurts
   And opens wide my shame.

3. For this man looks me through and through
   Beyond the outward form,
   It is my inner self that draws
   His love that's clean and warm,
   He does not judge nor pour abuse
   Yet in him I'm re-born.

4. And so I dare to meet his gaze
   That sees such good in me,
   I long to know integrity
   My guilty past set free,
   And drawn in love by his pure eyes
   My true self then I'll be.

Words and music by Margaret Evening

Appendix B: Bible Narratives and Themes for Dramatisation

A. *Old Testament*
   The Creation (Genesis chs. 1, 2)
   The Fall (Genesis ch. 3)
   Elijah and the widow of Zarephath (1 Kings ch. 17)
   Elijah on Mount Carmel (1 Kings ch. 18)
   Joseph and his brothers (Genesis ch. 37)
   David and Goliath (1 Samuel ch. 17)
   Scenes from the life of Solomon (1 Kings chs. 2–11)
   Scenes from Amos
   Scenes from Hosea
   Scenes from Jeremiah
   Scenes from Job
   Isaiah's vision and call (Isaiah ch. 6)
   Psalms
   Verses from Proverbs (e.g. 3: 25, 26; 17: 1; 18: 19, etc.)

B. *New Testament*
   The Good Samaritan (Luke 10: 25–37)
   The widow of Nain's son (Luke 7: 11–17)
   The storm on the lake (Luke 8: 22–25)
   The Word made flesh (John 1: 1–18)
   The feeding of the five thousand (Matthew 15: 29–39)
   The Nativity (Matthew 1: 18—2: 12; Luke 1: 26—2: 20)
   Gethsemane and Jesus's arrest (Luke 22: 39–62)
   Paul's conversion (Acts ch. 9)
   Paul in Philippi (Acts ch. 16)
   The Gadarene maniac restored (Luke 8: 26–39)
   The raising of Lazarus (John 11: 1–44)
   The man with the withered hand (Mark 3: 1–6)
   Zacchaeus (Luke 19: 1–10)

The healing of the centurion's son (Luke 7: 1–10)
The ten virgins (Matthew 25: 1–13)
The fruit of the Spirit (Galatians 5: 22–24)
The "I am" sayings in St. John's Gospel

C. *Themes*
    The Cross
    New Life
    Forgiveness
    Compassion
    War
    Machine Age
    Darkness and Light
    Turmoil and Peace
    Life Cycle
    Friendship
    Community
    Our Father
    Giving and Receiving
    Barriers
    Hands
    Eyes
    Scripts of dramatised Bible narratives are available from Christian
    Arts Project, 42 Caterham Road, Lewisham, London, SE13, and
    from The Religious Drama Society, George Bell House, Bishop's
    Hall, 8 Ayres Street, London SE1 1ES, where there is also a
    library of full-length and shorter plays and musicals. Religious
    verse, music, drama and thematic material are also available from
    Stainer and Bell (Galliard), 82 High Road, London N2 9PW.

Bibliography

Baldwin, F. and Whitehead, M. (ed.), *That Way and This—Poetry for Creative Dance* (Chatto and Windus Educational).

Bruce, Violet and Tooke, Joan, *Lord of the Dance* (Pergamon Press).

Cox, Harvey, *The Feast of Fools* (Harvard University Press).

Davies, J. G. (ed.), *Worship and Dance* (University of Birmingham Institute for the Study of Worship and Religious Architecture).

DeSola, Carla, *Learning Through Dance* (Paulist Press, New York).

Duriez, C. (ed.), *Making Eden Grow* (an anthology of Christian poetry) (Scripture Union).

Evening, Margaret, *Approaches to Religious Education* (Hodder and Stoughton).

Hobden, Sheila, *Explorations in Worship* (Lutterworth Educational).

Hodgson, J. and Richards, E., *Improvisation* (Methuen).

Keene, Sam, *To a Dancing God* (Harper and Row, New York).

Kelso, Andy, *Drama in Worship* (Grove Books, St. John's College, Bramcote, Notts. NG9 3DS).

Killinger, John, *Leave it to the Spirit* (S.C.M.).

Laban, R., *Modern Educational Dance* (3rd edition) (Macdonald and Evans).

Lion Handbook to the Bible (Lion Publishing).

Louf, A., *Teach us to Pray* (Darton, Longman and Todd).

Lowen, A., *Depression and the Body* (Collier Books, New York).

MacNutt, F., *Healing* (Ave Maria Press).

Male, D. A., *Approaches to Drama* (Unwin Educational Books).

Martin, W. and Vallins, G., *Exploration Drama* (Evans).

Musgrave, Horner A., *Movement, Voice and Speech* (Methuen).

North, Marion, *Introduction to Movement Study and Teaching* (Macdonald and Evans).

Oesterley, W., *The Sacred Dance: A Study in Comparative Folklore* (Cambridge University Press).

Preston, Valerie, *Handbook for Modern Educational Dance* (Preston).

Quoist, M., *Prayers of Life* (Gill and Son).

Reid, G., *The Gagging of God* (Hodder and Stoughton).

Russell, Joan, *Creative Dance in the Primary School* (Macdonald and Evans).

Russell, Joan, *Creative Dance in the Secondary School* (Macdonald and Evans).

Russell, Joan, *Modern Dance in Education* (Macdonald and Evans).

Schaeffer, F., *Art and the Bible* (Hodder and Stoughton).

Way, B., *Development through Drama* (Longmans).

Songbooks

Renewal Songbook (Fountain Trust).

Songs of Fellowship (Fountain Trust).

Sound of Living Waters, Pulkingham, B. and Harper, J. (Hodder and Stoughton).

Faith, Folk and Clarity, ed. P. Smith (Galliard Ltd.).

Faith, Folk and Festivity, ed. P. Smith (Galliard Ltd.).